ROYAL COURT

The Royal Court Theatre presents

THE FAITH MACHINE

by **Alexi Kaye Campbell**

THE FAITH MACHINE was first performed at the Royal Court Jerwood Theatre Downstairs,
Sloane Square, London on Thursday 25 August 2011.

Principal Sponsor Coutts

THE FAITH MACHINE

by Alexi Kaye Campbell

in order of appearance
Tom **Kyle Soller**
Sophie **Hayley Atwell**
Edward **Ian McDiarmid**
Patrick/Lawrence **Jude Akuwudike**
Tatyana **Bronagh Gallagher**
Sebastian **Alan Westaway**
Annie **Maya Wasowicz**
Agatha **Kezrena James**

Director **Jamie Lloyd**
Designer **Mark Thompson**
Lighting Designer **Neil Austin**
Music & Sound Designer **Alex Baranowski**
Video & Projection Designer **Lorna Heavey**
Casting Director **Amy Ball**
Assistant Director **Jacqui Honess-Martin**
Production Manager **Paul Handley**
Stage Manager **Sunita Hinduja**
Deputy Stage Manager **Fran O'Donnell**
Assistant Stage Manager **Lindsey Knight**
Costume Supervisor **Jackie Orton**
Dialect Coach **Penny Dyer**
Stage Management Work Placement **Sarah Harrison**
Set built by **Miraculous Engineering**
Set painted by **Kerry Jarrett**
Furniture Supplied by **Marcus Hall Props**

The Royal Court and Stage Management wish you to thank the following for their help with this production: Donmar Warehouse, My Big Fat Greek, Westminster Libraries.

THE COMPANY

ALEXI KAYE CAMPBELL (Writer)

As an actor Alexi has worked extensively in theatre across the country.

FOR THE ROYAL COURT: The Pride (& MCC, New York).

OTHER THEATRE INCLUDES: Apologia (Bush).

AWARDS INCLUDE: 2009 Critics Circle Prize for Most Promising Playwright for The Pride, 2009 John Whiting Award for Best New Play for The Pride, 2009 Olivier Award for Outstanding Achievement in an Affiliate Theatre for The Pride.

JUDE AKUWUDIKE (Patrick/Lawrence)

FOR THE ROYAL COURT: Marching for Fausa, The Recruiting Officer/Our Country's Good (with Out of Joint).

OTHER THEATRE INCLUDES: Passing Wind (Pulse Festival, New Wolsey Theatre/Talawa Theatre Company); Great Expectations (English Touring Theatre/Watford Palace Theatre); Othello (Glasgow Citizen's Theatre); The Rime of the Ancient Mariner (Young Vic/Southbank Centre); Iya-Ile (Tiata Fahodzi/Soho); Walking Waterfall (Tiata Fahodzi/Almeida); The Resistible Rise of Arturo Ui (Lyric Hammersmith); God in Ruins (RSC/Soho); Macbett, Macbeth, Pericles, The Winter's Tale, Luminosity (RSC); The Overwhelming (Out of Joint/National); Pericles (Shakespeare's Globe); Edmond, Henry V, Honk! The Ugly Duckling, The Machine Wreckers, Richard II, Ion (National); Not About Nightingales (National/Broadway); Young Hamlet (Young Vic); A Doll's House (Shared Experience); Nuremberg & 3 Responses, A Long Way From Home (Tricycle); Poor Superman (Traverse/Hampstead); Wiseguy Scapino (Theatre Clwyd); Light in the Village (Traverse); Death and the King's Horseman (Manchester Royal Exchange); The Relapse (Birmingham Rep); Master Harold and the Boys (Bristol Old Vic); The Fatherland (Riverside Studios); Moon on a Rainbow Shawl (Almeida); The Park (Sheffield Crucible).

TELEVISION INCLUDES: Law & Order, Holby City, The No. 1 Ladies Detective Agency, Moses Jones, Silent Witness, Bad Girls, The Last Detective, Ultimate Force, Roger Roger, The Mahabharata, Land of Dreams, Madmen and Specialists, Downtown Lagos, Virtual Murder, Bad Girl, Sam's Duck, The Bill, Between the Lines, A Likeness in Stone.

FILM INCLUDES: The Plan, The Tempest, Touched by a Stranger, Whisper the Way of the Child, Sahara, A World Apart.

RADIO INCLUDES: (Member of BBC Radio Drama Company 2010-2011) Anatomy of a Disappearance, Why is the Sky So Blue, World Service African Service, Nyama, Fences, Of Mice and Men, The Lady of Kingsland Waste, The Black Bono, Point of Departure, Dolly, Scoop, The Thebans, The No. 1 Ladies Detective Agency, Tide Race, Jero, Humans and Other Animals, A Thorn in the Flesh, Anthills of the Savannah, Out of Hours, Westway, Measure for Measure, The Other Side of the Truth.

HAYLEY ATWELL (Sophie)

THEATRE INCLUDES: A View from the Bridge (Duke of York's, West End); Major Barbara, Man of Mode (National); Women Beware Women (RSC); Prometheus Bound (IO).

TELEVISION INCLUDES: Any Human Heart, Pillars of the Earth, The Prisoner, Mansfield Park, Ruby in the Smoke, Fear of Fanny, The Line of Beauty.

FILM INCLUDES: I, Anna, Captain America: The First Avenger, The Duchess, Brideshead Revisited, How About You, Cassandra's Dream.

NEIL AUSTIN (Lighting Designer)

FOR THE ROYAL COURT: The Priory, Tusk Tusk, Flesh Wound, Trust.

OTHER THEATRE INCLUDES: The Cherry Orchard, Women Beware Women, The White Guard, London Assurance, England People Very Nice, Oedipus, Her Naked Skin, Philistines, The Man of Mode, Thérèse Raquin, The Seafarer, Henry IV Parts. 1 & 2, A Prayer for Owen Meany (National); The 25th Annual Putnam County Spelling Bee, King Lear, Passion, Red, A Streetcar Named Desire, Piaf, Parade, John Gabriel Borkman, Frost/Nixon, The Wild Duck, Caligula, After Miss Julie (Donmar); Hamlet, Madame de Sade and Twelfth Night (Donmar West End); King Lear, The Seagull, Much Ado About Nothing, Romeo & Juliet, King John, Two Gentlemen of Verona & Julius Caesar (RSC); Betty Blue Eyes, The Children's Hour, Dealer's Choice, No Man's Land, A Life in the Theatre, Japes (West End).

DANCE INCLUDES: Cinderella (New Adventures); As One & Rhapsody (Royal Ballet).

AWARDS INCLUDE: Winner of the 2011 Olivier Award for The White Guard and the 2010 Tony Award and Drama Desk Award for Red at the Golden Theatre on Broadway.

ALEX BARANOWSKI (Music & Sound Designer)

THEATRE INCLUDES: Hamlet, Frankenstein (National); Earthquakes in London (Headlong/National); Salt, Root, Roe (Donmar); The Merchant of Venice (RSC); Othello, Hobson's Choice (Sheffield Crucible); Rose (Pleasance); Herding Cats (Theatre Royal Bath).

DANCE: In the Dust (2Faced Dance/tour).

TELEVISION INCLUDES: Made in England, I Won't Go, NFA.

BRONAGH GALLAGHER (Tatyana)

FOR THE ROYAL COURT: Dublin Carol, Portia Coughlan (with Abbey Theatre, Dublin).

OTHER THEATRE INCLUDES: Every Good Boy Deserves Favour, Warhorse (National); Light, Street of Crocodiles (Complicite); The Rocky Horror PictureShow (SFX Centre Dublin); Caucasian Chalk Circle (Complicite/National/tour); The Iceman Cometh, A Crucial Week in the Life of a Grocer's Assistant, A Patriot Game (Abbey Theatre, Dublin).

TELEVISION INCLUDES: The Other Child, Pram Face, Field of Blood, The Accused, The Peter Serafinowicz Show, The Street, The Bill, Holby City, Poirot, Red and Blue, Sinners, The Fitz, Déjà vu, Cry Woolf, The Shadow of a Gunman, Ruffian Hearts, Over the Rainbow, You, Me and Marley, Flash McVeigh, Island of Strangers, Dear Sarah.

FILM INCLUDES: Albert Nobbs, Tamara Drewe, Sherlock Holmes, The Big I Am, Last Chance Harvey, Faintheart, Lecture 21, 13, Middletown, Tara Road, Tristan and Isolde, Spin the Bottle, Skagarrak, Thunderpants, Star Wars: The Phantom Menace, Divorcing Jack, Painted Angels, Pulp Fiction, Mary Reilly, The Commitments, This Year's Love, Thanks for the Memories, The Most Fertile Man in Ireland.

LORNA HEAVEY (Video & Projection Designer)

THEATRE INCLUDES: Romeo and Juliet, The Tempest, Speaking Like Magpies (RSC); Onassis, Speaking in Tongues (West End); Madame de Sade (Donmar West End); When the Rain Stops Falling (Almeida); Six Characters in Search of an Author (Headlong/Chichester/West End/Australia/UK tour); Macbeth (Headlong/Chichester/West End/Broadway); I Am Shakespeare (Chichester/UK tour); Aristo (Chichester); The Last Days of Judas Iscariot, Marianne Dreams (Almeida); King Lear (Headlong/Liverpool Everyman/Young Vic); Ten Tiny Toes (Liverpool Everyman/Shared Experience); Rough Crossings (Headlong/Liverpool Everyman/Lyric Hammersmith); The Caucasian Chalk Circle (National); Phaedra (Donmar); Faustus, Paradise Lost (Headlong); Vanishing Point (German Gym); Cleansed (Oxford Stage Company); Attempts on Her Life, The Waves (BAC); Genoa 01 (Complicite); Betrayal (Northampton).

SET, COSTUME & VIDEO: Branded (Old Vic); Nocturne (Almeida/Traverse); A Stitch in Time, Beautiful Beginnings, Hamlet Machine, Titus Andronicus (BAC).

OPERA INCLUDES: Turandot (ENO); Semper Dowland, The Corridor (Aldeburgh/QEH/Bregenz); Norma (Grange Park Opera); Mahabharata (Sadler's Wells); Dido and Aeneas (Northern Opera); Jeanne D'Arc (Santa Cecilia Academia, Rome); The Very Opera, Newsnight: The Opera (BAC).

TELEVISION INCLUDES: The Bendix Report, The Mighty Boosh.

FILM INCLUDES: Several Worlds, The Global Conditioned, Duet For One.

JACQUI HONESS MARTIN (Assistant Director)

AS ASSISTANT DIRECTOR FOR THE ROYAL COURT: Remembrance Day.

DIRECTING INCLUDES: Auricular (Theatre503); Smith (British Museum); Antigone (Walworth Council Chambers); The Country (Goldsmiths College); An Experiment with an Air Pump (Drama Centre).

AS ASSISTANT DIRECTOR, OTHER THEATRE INCLUDES: Arcadia (West End); Woyzeck (Cardboard Citizens).

AS PLAYWRIGHT: Tell Out My Soul (Summer Plays Festival at the Public Theater New York).

Jacqui is LIterary Associate for Menagerie Theatre Company.

KEZRENA JAMES (Agatha)

Kezrena is making her professional stage debut in The Faith Machine.

TELEVISION INCLUDES: Doctors, Crash.

JAMIE LLOYD (Director)

FOR THE ROYAL COURT: The Pride.

THEATRE INCLUDES: The 25th Annual Putnam County Spelling Bee, Passion, Polar Bears (Donmar); Piaf (Donmar/Vaudeville, West End/Teatro Liceo, Buenos Aires/Nuevo Teatro Alcala, Madrid); Salome (Headlong at Hampstead); The Little Dog Laughed (Garrick, West End); The Lover & The Collection (Comedy, West End); Elegies (Arts, West End) Eric's (Liverpool Everyman); The Caretaker (Sheffield Crucible/Tricycle).

AWARDS INCLUDE: Evening Standard Best Musical Award for Passion, Olivier Oustanding Achievement by an Affiliate Award for The Pride, Hugo Award for Best Director, Clarin Award for Best Musical Production, ADEET Award for Best Production all for Piaf, RSC Buzz Goodbody Director Award.

Jamie is an Associate Director of the Donmar Warehouse.

KYLE SOLLER (Tom)

FOR THE ROYAL COURT: Ice Cream (Caryl Churchill 70th Birthday Readings).

OTHER THEATRE INCLUDES: The Government Inspector, The Glass Menagerie (Young Vic); The Talented Mr Ripley (Northampton Royal & Derngate); The Glass Menagerie (Shared Experience); A Midsummer Night's Dream (Shakespeare's Globe Touring); The Beautiful People (Finborough).

RADIO INCLUDES: Goldfinger.

IAN McDIARMID (Edward)

FOR THE ROYAL COURT: Insignificance, Seduced, The Love of a Good Man, Hated Nightfall.

OTHER THEATRE INCLUDES: Emperor and Galilean, Tales from Hollywood (National); The Prince of Homburg, John Gabriel Borkman, Be Near Me [also adaptation], Henry IV (Donmar); Six Characters in Search of an Author (Headlong/West End/Chichester/Australian tour); Lear (Sheffield Crucible); The Embalmer, The Faith Healer [& New York], The Tempest, The Jew of Malta, The Doctor's Dilemma, Ivanov, Tartuffe, The Government Inspector, The Cenci, School for Wives, Volpone, The Saxon Shore, Creditors (Almeida, where Ian was joint Artistic Director of the Almeida Theatre from 1990 to 2002 with Jonathan Kent); Downchild, The Danton Affair, The Castle, Crimes in Hot Countries, The War Plays, The Party, The Merchant of Venice, Henry V, The Days of the Commune, Macbeth, That Good Between Us, Much Ado About Nothing, A fore Night Come, Schweyk in the Second World War, Dingo, Destiny, Measure for Measure (RSC); Edward II, The Country Wife, Don Carlos (Manchester Royal Exchange); The Black Prince (West End); Peer Gynt (Oxford Playhouse); Mephisto (Roundhouse).

TELEVISION INCLUDES: Margaret, City of Vice, Our Hidden Lives, Elizabeth I, Spooks, Charles II, Crime and Punishment, All the King's Men, Great Expectations, An Unsuitable Job for a Woman, Touching Evil, Rebecca, Hillsborough, Cold Lazarus, Karaoke, Annie: A Royal Adventure, Heart of Darkness, Selected Exits, The Young Indiana Jones Chronicles, Chernobyl: The Final Warning, Inspector Morse, Pity in History, The Nation's Health, The Professionals, Last Night Another Dissident, Macbeth, Creditors.

FILM INCLUDES: Star Wars Episodes I, II, III,IV, V, Sleepy Hollow, Restoration, Dirty Rotten Scoundrels, Gorky Park, Dragonslayer, Sir Henry at Rawlinson's End, The Awakening, Richard's Things, The Likely Lads.

AWARDS INCLUDE: 2006 Tony Awards Best Performance by a Featured Actor in a Play for Faith Healer, 2006 Critics' Circle Award for Faith Healer, 1982 Olivier Best Actor Award for Insignificance.

MARK THOMPSON (Designer)

FOR THE ROYAL COURT: Tribes, Piano Forte, The Woman Before, Wild East, Mouth to Mouth, Neverland, Six Degree of Separation, Hysteria, The Kitchen.

OTHER RECENT DESIGN INCLUDES: One Man, Two Guvnors, London Assurance, England People Very Nice, The Rose Tattoo, The Alchemist, Once in a Lifetime, Henry IV part I and II, The Duchess of Malfi; What The Butler Saw; Pericles; The Day I Stood Still; The Madness Of George III; The Wind In The Willows (National); Life x3 (National/Old Vic/Broadway); Children's Hour (West End); La Bête (West End/Broadway); Arcadia (National/Lincoln Center NY); Rope; Volpone; Betrayal; Party Time; Butterfly Kiss (Almeida); God of Carnage (Gielgud Theatre, Broadway); Female of the Species (Vaudeville Theatre); Joseph and the Amazing Technicolor Dreamcoat (Adelphi Theatre); Kean (UK tour/Apollo Theatre); And Then There Were None (Gielgud Theatre); Funny Girl (Chichester Festival Theatre); Mamma Mia! (Prince of Wales Theatre/Prince Edward Theatre/Toronto/US Tour/ Broadway/ Japan/ Germany/Australia); Bombay Dreams (Apollo Victoria/Broadway). Costumes for Uncle Vanya and Twelfth Night (Donmar Warehouse/B.A.M.); Measure for Measure; The Wizard of Oz; Much Ado About Nothing; The Comedy of Errors; Hamlet, The Unexpected Man (RSC); Insignificance, Company, The Front Page (Donmar); The Blue Room (Donmar/Broadway).

OTHER THEATRE INCLUDES: The Lady in the Van (Queen's Theatre); Dr Dolittle (Hammersmith Apollo); Blast (Hammersmith Apollo & Broadway); Art (Wyndham Theatre & Broadway). Set only for Follies (Broadway).

OPERA INCLUDES: Carmen (L'Opera Comique); Macbeth, Queen of Spades (Metropolitan Opera, New York); Falstaff (Scottish Opera); Peter Grimes (Opera North); Ariadne auf Naxoœ (Salzburg); Il Viaggio a Reims (Royal Opera House); Hanseland Gretal (Sydney Opera House); The Two Widows (ENO). Costumes only for Montag Aus Licht (La Scala, Milan).

BALLET: Don Quixote (Royal Ballet).

FILM: Costume design for The Madness of King George.

AWARDS: Mark is the winner of 4 Olivier Awards and 2 Critics Circle Awards.

MAYA WASOWICZ (Annie)

THEATRE INCLUDES: Design for Living (Old Vic); Death of a Salesman (West Yorkshire Playhouse); Twelfth Night (RSC).

TELEVISION INCLUDES: Waking the Dead, Mutual Friends.

FILM INCLUDES: Huge.

ALAN WESTAWAY (Sebastian)

THEATRE INCLUDES: The Winslow Boy (Salisbury Playhouse); Rabbit (Trafalgar Studios & E59st Theatre NY); Singer (Tricycle); Romeo & Juliet, As You Like It (Regent's Park); Sexual Perversity, Twelfth Night (Sheffield Crucible); John Wayne Principle (Nuffield); Julius Caesar (Manchester Royal Exchange); The King of Prussia (Minerva, Chichester); The Clandestine Marriage (Watermill, Newbury); Barefoot in the Park (Watford Palace, Royal Northampton); Pera Pelas (Gate); Faithful Dealing (Soho); Revenger's Tragedy, The Pelican (Orange Tree); Merchant of Venice (Library Theatre, Manchester).

TELEVISION INCLUDES: The Borgias, Skins, Holby City, Peep Show, Silent Witness, D-Day, Casualty, Eastenders, Two Pints of Lager and a Packet of Crisps, Doctors, The Ricky Gervais Show, Headless, The Bill, The Hello Girls, Peak Practice, In Tandem.

FILM INCLUDES: Land of the Blind, D-Day, Stratosphere Girl, Little Scars, Virtual Sexuality, Double Heartbeat, Grandma's Footsteps, Sleeper, Deb, To Sleep.

THE ENGLISH STAGE COMPANY
AT THE ROYAL COURT THEATRE

*'For me the theatre is really a religion or way of life.
You must decide what you feel the world is about
and what you want to say about it, so that everything
in the theatre you work in is saying the same thing
... A theatre must have a recognisable attitude. It will
have one, whether you like it or not.'*

George Devine, first artistic director of the
English Stage Company: notes for an unwritten
book.

photo: Stephen Cummiskey

As Britain's leading national company dedicated to new work, the Royal Court Theatre produces new plays of the highest quality, working with writers from all backgrounds, and asking questions about who we are and the world in which we live.

"The Royal Court has been at the centre of British cultural life for the past 50 years, an engine room for new writing and constantly transforming the theatrical culture." Stephen Daldry

Since its foundation in 1956, the Royal Court has presented premieres by almost every leading contemporary British playwright, from John Osborne's Look Back in Anger to Caryl Churchill's A Number and Tom Stoppard's Rock 'n' Roll. Just some of the other writers to have chosen the Royal Court to premiere their work include Edward Albee, John Arden, Richard Bean, Samuel Beckett, Edward Bond, Leo Butler, Jez Butterworth, Martin Crimp, Ariel Dorfman, Stella Feehily, Christopher Hampton, David Hare, Eugène Ionesco, Ann Jellicoe, Terry Johnson, Sarah Kane, David Mamet, Martin McDonagh, Conor McPherson, Joe Penhall, Lucy Prebble, Mark Ravenhill, Simon Stephens, Wole Soyinka, Polly Stenham, David Storey, Debbie Tucker Green, Arnold Wesker and Roy Williams.

"It is risky to miss a production there." Financial Times

In addition to its full-scale productions, the Royal Court also facilitates international work at a grass roots level, developing exchanges which bring young writers to Britain and sending British writers, actors and directors to work with artists around the world. The research and play development arm of the Royal Court Theatre, The Studio, finds the most exciting and diverse range of new voices in the UK. The Studio runs play-writing groups including the Young Writers Programme, Critical Mass for black, Asian and minority ethnic writers and the biennial Young Writers Festival. For further information, go to http://www.royalcourttheatre.com/playwriting.

"Yes, the Royal Court is on a roll. Yes, Dominic Cooke has just the genius and kick that this venue needs... It's fist-bitingly exciting." Independent

ROYAL COURT SUPPORTERS

The Royal Court is able to offer its unique playwriting and audience development programmes because of significant and longstanding partnerships with the organisations that support it.

Coutts is the Principal Sponsor of the Royal Court. The Genesis Foundation supports the Royal Court's work with International Playwrights. Theatre Local is sponsored by Bloomberg. The Jerwood Charitable Foundation supports new plays by playwrights through the Jerwood New Playwrights series. The Artistic Director's Chair is supported by a lead grant from The Peter Jay Sharp Foundation, contributing to the activities of the Artistic Director's office. Over the past ten years the BBC has supported the Gerald Chapman Fund for directors.

The Harold Pinter Playwright's Award is given annually by his widow, Lady Antonia Fraser, to support a new commission at the Royal Court.

PUBLIC FUNDING
Arts Council England, London
British Council
European Commission Representation in the UK

CHARITABLE DONATIONS
American Friends of the Royal Court
Martin Bowley Charitable Trust
The Brim Foundation*
Gerald Chapman Fund
City Bridge Trust
Cowley Charitable Trust
The H and G de Freitas Charitable Trust
The Dorset Foundation
The John Ellerman Foundation
The Eranda Foundation
Genesis Foundation
J Paul Getty Jnr Charitable Trust
The Golden Bottle Trust
The Haberdashers' Company
Paul Hamlyn Foundation
Jerwood Charitable Foundation
Marina Kleinwort Charitable Trust
The Leathersellers' Company
John Lyon's Charity
The Andrew W Mellon Foundation
The Laura Pels Foundation*
Jerome Robbins Foundation*
Rose Foundation
Royal Victoria Hall Foundation
The Dr Mortimer & Theresa Sackler Foundation
The Peter Jay Sharp Foundation*
The Steel Charitable Trust
John Thaw Foundation
The Garfield Weston Foundation

CORPORATE SUPPORTERS & SPONSORS
BBC
Bloomberg
Coutts
Ecosse Films
French Wines
Grey London
Kudos Film & Television
MAC
Moët & Chandon
Oakley Capital Limited
Sky Arts
Smythson of Bond Street

BUSINESS ASSOCIATES, MEMBERS & BENEFACTORS
Auerbach & Steele Opticians
Bank of America Merrill Lynch
Hugo Boss
Lazard
Louis Vuitton
Oberon Books
Savills
Vanity Fair

DEVELOPMENT ADVOCATES
John Ayton
Elizabeth Bandeen
Tim Blythe
Anthony Burton
Sindy Caplan
Sarah Chappatte
Cas Donald (Vice Chair)
Allie Esiri
Celeste Fenichel
Anoushka Healy
Emma Marsh (Chair)
William Russell
Deborah Shaw Marquardt (Vice Chair)
Nick Wheeler
Daniel Winterfeldt

Supported by
ARTS COUNCIL ENGLAND

FOR THE ROYAL COURT

Royal Court Theatre, Sloane Square, London SW1W 8AS
Tel: 020 7565 5050 Fax: 020 7565 5001
info@royalcourttheatre.com, www.royalcourttheatre.com

Artistic Director **Dominic Cooke**
Associate Directors **Simon Godwin, Jeremy Herrin*, Sacha Wares***
Artistic Associate **Emily McLaughlin***
Diversity Associate **Ola Animashawun***
Education Associate **Lynne Gagliano***
PA to the Artistic Director **Pamela Wilson**

Literary Manager **Christopher Campbell**
Senior Reader **Nicola Wass****
Literary Assistant **Marcelo Dos Santos**
Studio Administrator **Clare McQuillan**
Writers' Tutor **Leo Butler***
Pearson Playwright **DC Moore ^**

Associate Director International **Elyse Dodgson**
International Projects Manager **Chris James**
International Assistant **William Drew**

Casting Director **Amy Ball**
Casting Assistant **Lotte Hines**

Head of Production **Paul Handley**
JTU Production Manager **Tariq Rifaat**
Production Administrator **Rebecca Maltby**
Head of Lighting **Matt Drury**
Lighting Deputy **Stephen Andrews**
Lighting Assistants **Katie Pitt, Jack Williams**
Lighting Board Operator **Jack Champion**
Head of Stage **Steven Stickler**
Stage Deputy **Dan Lockett**
Stage Chargehand **Lee Crimmen**
Chargehand Carpenter **Richard Martin**
Head of Sound **David McSeveney**
Sound Deputy **Alex Caplen**
Sound Operator **Sam Charleston**
Head of Costume **Iona Kenrick**
Costume Deputy **Jackie Orton**
Wardrobe Assistant **Pam Anson**

Executive Director **Kate Horton**
General Manager **Catherine Thornborrow**
Administrative Assistant **Holly Handel**

Head of Finance & Administration **Helen Perryer**
Senior Finance & Administration Officer **Martin Wheeler**
Finance Officer **Rachel Harrison***
Finance & Administration Assistant **Tessa Rivers**

Head of Marketing & Sales **Becky Wootton**
Acting Marketing Manager **Helen Slater**
Press & Public Relations Officer **Anna Evans**
Communications Assistant **Ruth Hawkins**
Communications Interns **Anoushka Arden, Hannah Clapham**
Sales Manager **Kevin West**
Deputy Sales Manager **Liam Geoghegan**
Box Office Sales Assistants **Joe Hodgson, Carla Kingham*, Stephen Laughton*, Helen Murray*, Ciara O'Toole, Helen Preddy***

Head of Development **Gaby Styles**
Senior Development Manager **Hannah Clifford**
Development Manager **Lucy Buxton**
Development Officer **Penny Saward**

Theatre Manager **Bobbie Stokes**
Front of House Manager **Rachel Dudley**
Events Manager **Joanna Ostrom**
Duty Managers **Fiona Clift*, Elinor Keber***
Front of House Assistant **Deirdre Lennon***
Bar & Food Manager **Sami Rifaat**
Deputy Bar & Food Manager **Ali Christian**
Interim Head Chef **Tim Tenner**
Sous Chef **Paulino Chuitcheu**
Bookshop Manager **Simon David**
Bookshop Assistants **Vanessa Hammick*, Tom Clancy***
Stage Door/Reception **Paul Lovegrove, Tyrone Lucas**

Thanks to all of our ushers and bar staff.

^This theatre has the support of the Pearson Playwrights' Scheme sponsored by the Peggy Ramsay Foundation.

** The post of Senior Reader is supported by NoraLee & Jon Sedmak through the American Friends of the Royal Court Theatre.

‡The post of the Trainee Director is supported by the BBC writersroom.

* Part-time.

ENGLISH STAGE COMPANY

President
Dame Joan Plowright CBE

Honorary Council
Sir Richard Eyre CBE
Alan Grieve CBE
Martin Paisner CBE

Council
Chairman **Anthony Burton**
Vice Chairman **Graham Devlin CBE**

Members
Jennette Arnold OBE
Judy Daish
Sir David Green KCMG
Joyce Hytner OBE
Stephen Jeffreys
Wasfi Kani OBE
Phyllida Lloyd CBE
James Midgley
Sophie Okonedo OBE
Alan Rickman
Anita Scott
Katharine Viner
Stewart Wood

Autumn 2011

Jerwood Theatre Downstairs

13 Oct – 19 Nov

jumpy
by April De Angelis

2 Dec – 14 Jan

haunted child
by Joe Penhall

Jerwood Theatre Upstairs

11 Oct – 5 Nov

bang bang bang
by Stella Feehily

Co-production with the Royal Court, Out of Joint,
The Curve, Leicester, The Octagon, Bolton and
Salisbury Playhouse.

25 Nov – 23 Dec

the westbridge
by Rachel De-lahay

020 7565 5000
www.royalcourttheatre.com

THE FAITH MACHINE

Alexi Kaye Campbell

In memory of Stephen Tredre

'Life is lived forwards but understood backwards'

Søren Kierkegaard

Characters

in order of speaking

TOM, *ages from twenty-four to thirty-seven during the play, American*

SOPHIE, *ages from twenty-two to thirty-four during the play, English*

EDWARD, *in his seventies, English*

PATRICK, *in his forties, Black Kenyan*

TATYANA, *in her thirties or forties, Russian*

SEBASTIAN, *in his forties, Chilean*

LAWRENCE, *ages from thirties to forties, Black British*

ANNIE, *in her thirties, American*

AGATHA, *seventeen*

The roles of Patrick and Lawrence are to be played by the same actor.

Bold letters in the Russian pronunciation indicate stress.

This text went to press before the end of rehearsals and so may differ slightly from the play as performed.

ACT ONE

Scene One

2001

New York radio: something about the weather, it being a sunny September morning, maybe a traffic update.

Lights up:

The bedroom of TOM*'s apartment in downtown Manhattan. A slick, expensive place, sparsely but tastefully furnished – the home of a young, successful man.*

Early morning. TOM *is still in his dressing gown but gets dressed during the scene.* SOPHIE *is half-dressed. She is putting things into a suitcase. She packs throughout the scene.*

TOM. So what are you asking me to do?

She doesn't answer.

Because I'm sorry, but this is who I am. I work in this city, I live in this world. I am a part of it.

SOPHIE. We both are.

TOM. But I have a feeling that if you finish packing that bag – will you please stop, just put that down, stop packing that bag, will you, GIVE ME THAT AT LEAST, put the fucking – whatever that is – put it down.

She stops packing.

Thank you. That if you finish packing that bag, that if you leave New York this afternoon, if you go back to London, then fuck me I don't know where that leaves us, but I don't know –

SOPHIE. I need to think.

TOM. – if we can ever pick things up is what I'm saying, *resume* things, because if you really want me to be honest here –

SOPHIE. You know I do.

TOM. – well, to be honest I feel judged, *vilified* in some way, frowned upon, Jesus, yes, just continuously judged –

SOPHIE. By me?

She resumes packing her bag.

TOM. – and I'm sorry I'm not Jesus or Mahatma Gandhi or fuck knows who you want me to be –

SOPHIE. I want you to be you.

TOM. – but the fact is, Sophie, this is who I am, and you just have to *accept* that: a good man who happens to work in a field that you – fuck me, I don't know, *disapprove* of – a good man who just happens to work in advertising.

SOPHIE. I know you work in advertising, Tom, I know how things evolved –

TOM. It's what I do.

SOPHIE. – to what they are, and I know that the world needs to keep turning.

TOM. Oh, you do?

SOPHIE. Buying, selling, supply, demand.

TOM. And it's advertising that helped us move into this apartment –

SOPHIE. I liked Brooklyn.

TOM. – and that happily funded your postgraduate degree at Columbia.

SOPHIE. My inheritance could have paid for that.

TOM. It's all you fucking have.

SOPHIE. But there's a line, Tom. That's all. A line.

TOM. A line?

SOPHIE. Let's call it the Fletcher line.

TOM. Jesus.

Pause.

SOPHIE. Why did you take the Fletcher contract, Tom?

TOM. Because it's a means to an end.

SOPHIE. Why did you chase it?

TOM. Because it opens doors. Because another two contracts like it and I can stop working. And then fuck knows, maybe we *can* save the world –

SOPHIE. You're believing your own sound bites.

TOM. Build a fucking orphanage in Kenya, Vietnam.

SOPHIE. 'It's a means to an end.'

TOM. Fucking Mozambique.

SOPHIE. Jesus, Tom.

TOM. I mean, I have been working so fucking hard –

SOPHIE. *What for?*

TOM. Joe Ikeman called me yesterday and said, 'It's unheard of.'

SOPHIE. I'm sure it is.

TOM. He said, 'For someone who's been writing copy for less than three years to head the Fletcher account is amazing. It's history, advertising history.'

SOPHIE. '*The Power to Heal*'. It's pithy, I'll give you that. No wonder they liked your pitch, you should be proud.

TOM. Well, fuck you, Sophie, I am proud and you know I too wish we lived in some idyllic, some, no, what's the word, *utopian* world, yes, if we lived in a fucking utopia then I would be earning a hell of a lot of money –

SOPHIE. We don't need a lot.

TOM. – for writing confessional novels about dysfunctional childhoods, but I'm afraid we don't, we live in the real world –

SOPHIE. Is that what it's called?

TOM. – and the real word is harsh, and cruel and full of compromise.

SOPHIE. Leave the ad-speak at work, I beg you. Let's keep something untouched.

Pause. EDWARD *walks into the room: they cannot see him.*

TOM. And this is all about your father, by the way.

SOPHIE. No, it isn't.

TOM. And I keep saying to myself it's part of the mourning process, one of the phases, you know, what do they say, the seven stages of mourning –

SOPHIE. Five.

TOM. So this is maybe stage five because ever since he died he's like, I don't know like, he's in this bedroom with us –

SOPHIE. The bedroom?

TOM. And I can understand it, I mean, the man was exceptional in every possible way, visionary and courageous and spiritually ambitious –

SOPHIE. He was.

EDWARD. Thank you, darling.

TOM. But having him in our bedroom twenty-four-seven isn't exactly conducive to a healthy relationship.

SOPHIE. Are you saying I can't think for myself?

EDWARD. His socks are inside out.

TOM. I'm saying that you need to let go of certain dogmatic ways of seeing things which are filled to the brim with the love of humanity, whatever you want to call it – but which are also incompatible with the world we happen to be living in right now and – dare, I say it, ever so slightly obsolete and archaic.

EDWARD. Ethics?

SOPHIE. Ethics are obsolete and archaic?

TOM. So it really is time to let him go.

EDWARD. Oh, he provokes.

SOPHIE. Your socks are inside out.

Pause. He takes them off, puts them on again the right way round.

EDWARD. Show him the file.

SOPHIE. The file.

TOM. What file?

EDWARD. You've done your homework, you have the evidence. Show him the file.

SOPHIE. I've put together a file.

TOM. What file?

EDWARD. Show it to him, Sophie.

She walks over to the bedside table and opens the drawer. She takes out a thin cardboard file.

SOPHIE. The Fletcher file.

TOM. First we had the Fletcher line, now we have the Fletcher file. I'm intrigued.

EDWARD. That's a start.

TOM. And pray tell, what is this Fletcher file?

EDWARD. Read it to him.

SOPHIE. Cases, case histories, that kind of thing. Clippings, articles, the odd opinion piece. Gleaned from the internet mostly, and the library.

TOM. You've been busy.

EDWARD. Very.

SOPHIE. I know you're late for work so I'll keep it brief.

TOM. How considerate.

She opens the file and starts going through the clippings.

SOPHIE. Most of it I won't bore you with, endless examples of corruption, bribery, fiddling, what not, unethical this, unethical that, pretty much what you'd expect from one of the world's leading pharmaceuticals.

TOM. Okay.

SOPHIE. I won't even go into the spurious marketing of four drugs including –

TOM. Detoxtrin.

SOPHIE. – thank you, and Flaxorin which led to seven deaths including that of a six-year-old epileptic girl in Minnesota last year, which followed the wilful suppression of unfavourable studies –

TOM. There was a settlement –

SOPHIE. Yes, I'm sure her parents are living in splendour somewhere –

TOM. Remind me again why we're doing this.

EDWARD. Because you need to hear it.

SOPHIE. Or the continuous promotion of various drugs for non-approved uses, including, of course, the misbranding of Fenerak, the destroying of documents pertinent to the investigation being a detail I'll just skim over in this instance –

TOM. What is your point?

SOPHIE. And instead I'll just focus if you don't mind on the one case –

TOM. Uganda.

SOPHIE. – choosing it perhaps – because of the constrictions of time and the urgency to communicate my grievances – in a representative, if you like, way –

TOM. Representative?

SOPHIE. – as the most telling example I mean of this company's – excuse me, of your new client's – *character* and in order to focus some of the questions I'd like to ask you on just this one case, using it as a point of reference –

TOM. Go on, then.

SOPHIE. – as a launch pad, if you like, for me to discover –

TOM. Interrogate.

SOPHIE. – who it is I'm living with these days.

TOM. Fuck you, Sophie.

EDWARD. Read it to him.

Pause. She takes a deep breath before launching into it. She reads from a clipping, interjecting from time to time with her own remarks.

SOPHIE. 'Two years ago, in 1999, an outbreak of measles, cholera and bacterial meningitis occurred in a region of Eastern Uganda –

TOM. I know all this.

EDWARD. Louder, with feeling.

SOPHIE (*increasing in volume and intensity*). About one hundred and twenty miles north of the capital, Kampala. Representatives of Fletcher's were there within a fortnight to assist' –

EDWARD. Assist!

SOPHIE. That's the word it uses – *assist* – 'the affected population. An experimental antibiotic, Maloflaxacin, was administered to approximately three hundred children. Local officials reported that more than one hundred of those children died from infection within two days of ingesting the drug, whilst the great majority of the rest developed mental and physical deformities.

TOM. I said I know all this.

SOPHIE. According to consistent reports of various witnesses, Fletcher administered the Maloflaxacin *without* parental consent.'

TOM. It's going to court.

SOPHIE. I know, here it is, there's more: 'In the lawsuits, Fletcher is accused of using the outbreak to perform unapproved human testing as well as allegedly under-dosing a control group –

EDWARD. *Unapproved human testing.*

SOPHIE. – being treated with traditional antibiotics in order to skew the results of the trial in favor of Maloflaxacin.'

TOM. Would you please tell me where the fuck this is leading?

SOPHIE. It's leading, I suppose, to the fundamental question, Tom, which is not 'What are you doing working with these people?' or 'How do you feel in your heart helping this company promote an image of themselves which is at the very least dishonest?' or not even 'In abetting a criminal – '

TOM. Abetting?

EDWARD. That's the word.

SOPHIE. ' – do you in fact become an accomplice to the crimes of murder, perjury, corruption…'

TOM. For fuck's sake.

SOPHIE. But the question it's leading to, the essential question to which I need to know the answer, Tom, if we are to continue living together, trying to form a *home* together, is quite simple really and the question is –

TOM. You're unbelievable.

EDWARD. 'Who are you?'

SOPHIE. Is 'Who are you, Tom?' Who are you? Who are you?

TOM. Who am I?

Pause.

SOPHIE. Are you, for instance – and this is just one possible strand, one of many directions we can choose to go in – are you, for instance, a *racist*, Tom?

TOM. How can you even ask that?

SOPHIE. And as a racist I don't necessarily mean someone who walks around in a hooded white top with – I don't know – a pitchfork or a blazing torch in his hand – no, that would be crude, too obvious –

TOM. How can you fucking ask that?

SOPHIE. But more someone who believes that the life of a child born in another part of the world, who just happens to be of a different ' colour and belongs to a whole other socio-economic group from his dear self, is not quite worth the same as that of a child living in, let's say, I don't know, Hartford, Connecticut or Paris, France?

TOM. The fact that you even –

SOPHIE. Because it feels to me, Tom, that your new friends at Fletcher do make that distinction, they make it most emphatically by choosing to send their teams to Uganda in order to 'assist' in this particular way, knowing full well that they're using those children as laboratory animals all in the pursuit of nothing more than the bottom dollar.

TOM. You're simplifying things.

SOPHIE. Because their lives are expendable, worthless, replaceable.

EDWARD. Simplifying things?

TOM. Things don't change overnight.

EDWARD. *The best lack all conviction.*

SOPHIE. Things don't change at all, Tom, unless you force them.

Pause.

TOM. So what are you asking me to do? I don't have the time to sit here in this room having abstract conversations about –

EDWARD. Abstract?

SOPHIE. They're *abstract*?

TOM. – about the choices we make, about moral decisions, about what it means to survive in a particular society –

EDWARD. To *thrive* in a particular society.

SOPHIE. Nothing abstract about what we're talking about.

TOM. Of which we are all a part, like it or not, in which we all try to do the best we can –

EDWARD. Do we?

TOM. – realistically, I mean, within the confines, the constrictions of the real world –

SOPHIE. There it is again, that real world you insist on referring to –

EDWARD. You create that world, Tom, you're creating it now.

SOPHIE. – as if you're implying you're trapped in it, some hapless prisoner –

TOM. Realistically, practically, what are you asking me to do?

SOPHIE. – instead of an active, conscious member of it who has the power not only to question it but to challenge, oppose, radicalise and reconstruct it.

TOM. Realistically.

SOPHIE. Because that is the person I thought you were.

EDWARD. *The Power to Heal.*

TOM. Jesus.

Pause.

EDWARD. Test him.

SOPHIE. I want you to go in today and turn it down. Turn down the Fletcher contract.

EDWARD. Test his mettle.

TOM. You what?

SOPHIE. I want you to go into work today and tell Roger Hartmann that you are turning down the Fletcher contract. That you don't want anything to do with it.

TOM. An ultimatum.

SOPHIE. Other jobs, fine, other contracts. But not this one.

TOM. So you're blackmailing me.

SOPHIE. Am I?

TOM. I think that's what it's called. I think you're saying 'Turn down the Fletcher contract or I'm going to England and there's a good chance I may not return.'

EDWARD. That is what she's saying.

TOM. Well, I can't do it, even if I wanted to.

SOPHIE. Why not?

TOM. Not that I do because I will not be blackmailed, Sophie, held to fucking ransom.

SOPHIE. Why can't you do it?

TOM. I can't turn around after eight months of prepping for the fucking thing and say, 'You know what, Roger, I have ethical concerns.'

SOPHIE. I don't want to go, Tom. But the simple fact is that if you go ahead with the Fletcher contract, I don't know if I'll be able to live with you any more.

TOM. Be careful what you're saying, Sophie.

SOPHIE. I know what I'm saying, Tom.

TOM. Be careful what you're saying.

EDWARD. She knows what she's saying.

TOM. You fucking wait till now –

SOPHIE. You knew how I felt about it.

TOM. And you fucking threaten me –

SOPHIE. We talked about it in the summer, when it first came up –

TOM. Blackmail me –

SOPHIE. You knew what I thought –

TOM. Not like this, you never said –

SOPHIE. You always knew.

TOM. Not that you were going to put me in this position.

EDWARD. Because you wanted him to do it himself.

SOPHIE. And if nothing else, I mean, even if you can't dig deep enough to find some kind of regret, I don't know, something in you like a conscience, something stirring deep inside your soul that reminds you that there are inescapable –

EDWARD. Ancient.

SOPHIE. Inescapable ancient truths nagging at you, tearing at you, saying over and over again –

EDWARD. You are your brother's keeper, Tom.

SOPHIE. – that you are your brother's keeper, Tom, but if nothing else, then realise at least that this constant injustice, *racism*, these laws that favour only the fortunate –

TOM. Jesus Christ.

SOPHIE. – will come back to you –

EDWARD. A hundredfold.

SOPHIE. – a thousandfold, Tom, like some fucking karmic boomerang, because everything, every choice you make has its consequences. Whether or not you're consciously aware of it.

Pause.

That's all.

A long pause.

TOM. You're mad, Sophie. I love you so much but you're completely mad. If you feel that you have to go –

SOPHIE. I don't want to.

TOM. – then you must go. But I can't drop the job. Not now. I *won't* drop the job. I'd like it if you stayed and supported me but if you…

SOPHIE. *Please, Tom.*

TOM. I can't. I won't. End of.

Pause.

EDWARD. *The blood-dimmed tide is loosed.*

And then, suddenly, the sound of a jet engine can be heard approaching. It increases in volume and then for a second, as it passes overhead, it is deafening.

Just as suddenly, silence.

Blackout…

Scene Two

1998

…or maybe a single light remains on EDWARD: *he stays in the middle of the space and the scene changes around him. The apartment fades away and we are transported to* EDWARD's *house on the island of Patmos in Greece. In sharp contrast to the slick minimalism of the first scene, this space is warm, colourful, soulful. It is a terrace but at the back of the space we see some of the interior: a room full of books, pictures, strange and beautiful objects – many of them with religious or tribal significance – collected from various trips and experiences around the world. The living museum of* EDWARD's *soul.*

As if it can't contain itself, some of the house's objects seem to have overspilt onto the terrace and have invaded some of the outside space as well: a pile or two of books, a picture leaning against an outside wall, an armchair, a stack of old newspapers tied with strings. At the centre of the terrace stands a large oak table, the kind of table around which the whole day is spent. This is the home of a brilliant, eccentric, slightly chaotic polymath.

It is an early evening in September. EDWARD *stands on one side of the terrace, and directly opposite him stands* PATRICK. *He holds a briefcase and is slightly out of breath; he has just arrived.*

EDWARD. You found me.

PATRICK. Persistence.

EDWARD. I'm warning you, I'm not a happy man.

PATRICK. We're not going to let go of you as easily as that.

EDWARD. You've come in vain.

PATRICK. Hello, Edward.

EDWARD. Patrick.

PATRICK. That was a dramatic exit you made.

EDWARD. I was feeling dramatic.

PATRICK. Well, you certainly made an impression. 1998 will be remembered as a vintage year.

EDWARD. Plenty of blood and gore but this time it was the gays who were being thrown to the lions and the Christians who were doing the cheering.

PATRICK. I wouldn't describe it like that.

EDWARD. I use the word Christians, of course, with just a tinge of irony.

PATRICK. Difficult days.

EDWARD. And then there were the ones sitting firmly on the fence. They're the worst of the lot, Patrick.

EDWARD *pours* PATRICK *a glass of ouzo from a bottle on the table. Hands it to him.*

I wish I could say this was unexpected.

PATRICK. Athens is halfway between London and Nairobi. And then there was the ferry from Piraeus.

EDWARD. I thought you might turn up.

PATRICK. But it's a fleeting visit.

EDWARD. What a shame.

PATRICK. The fact is that my flight leaves Athens for Nairobi tomorrow evening. And in order to catch it I have to be back on the ferry – the same one that brought me here – first thing tomorrow morning.

EDWARD. Is that all you've given yourself?

PATRICK. You know what I'm like.

EDWARD. An optimist, yes.

PATRICK. A man of faith. We both are.

EDWARD. Are we?

PATRICK. Stubborn and full of hope.

EDWARD. Full of something.

PATRICK. Are you turning cynical on me, Edward?

EDWARD. Trouble is we don't believe in the same God any more.

Pause.

PATRICK. The Archbishop sent me. Not that it was hard to
convince me.

EDWARD. He's cleverer than I thought.

PATRICK. Why's that?

EDWARD. Because he knows there's only one man who could ever
come close.

PATRICK. A compliment.

EDWARD. But not nearly close enough.

Pause.

PATRICK. Patmos. Your hideaway.

EDWARD. And now my retirement home. You've never been to the
island before?

PATRICK. It's my first time in Greece.

EDWARD. Welcome.

PATRICK. Thank you.

EDWARD. To the land where Hebrew prophecy and Greek
rationalism first entered their inevitable and complicated marriage.

PATRICK. Yes.

EDWARD. You don't even have time to visit the cave where John is
alleged to have had his revelations.

PATRICK. Sadly not.

EDWARD. Half a kilometre down the road. Past the man selling pistachios and beach towels.

PATRICK. I'll get to the point. You can't leave, Edward. The Church needs you. Now more than ever.

EDWARD. Does it indeed.

TATYANA walks on carrying a tray laden with plates and cutlery. When she speaks, she jumps between English and Russian.

TATYANA. Did you eat the smokey salmon, Edward?

EDWARD. Not that I recall.

TATYANA. This morning it was big. Now it is small. And I do not have enough food. I have only beetroot salad, potato salad, and the meatballs.

EDWARD. Is that all?

TATYANA (*noticing* PATRICK). Who is this?

EDWARD. This, Tatyana, is the Reverend Patrick Mwangi, Bishop of Keriko.

TATYANA. I am Tatyana.

PATRICK. Hello, Tatyana.

EDWARD. Patrick and I met when I was living in Kenya many years ago.

PATRICK. We have remained friends over the years.

EDWARD. Against the odds.

TATYANA. You are eating the dinner with us?

PATRICK. Well, I –

EDWARD. We can squeeze him in.

TATYANA. Не хватит еды. [*Pronounced: 'Nyeh khvah-teet yay-dee.' Meaning: 'There is not enough food.'*]

PATRICK. If that's all right with you.

EDWARD. We'll manage.

TATYANA. I make more salad.

EDWARD. Do that.

PATRICK. But really don't go to any trouble.

EDWARD. We have to send him on his way well fed and with a smile on his face.

PATRICK. Now you're talking.

EDWARD. Even if all that's making him smile is a belly full of beetroot.

TATYANA. What are you talking about?

EDWARD. So yes please, one more place at our table. And the man will need a bed too. He can sleep in the downstairs room.

TATYANA. Как будто у меня без этого работы мало.
[*Prounounced 'Kak butto u menia bez etava rabotu malo.' Meaning: 'As if I don't have enough work already.'*]

She leaves.

EDWARD. She's Russian. From the Ukraine.

PATRICK. Formidable is the word that comes to mind.

EDWARD. I can think of a few more.

PATRICK. Forty-five years, Edward.

EDWARD. Forty-seven.

PATRICK. Of dedication.

EDWARD. You haven't even done your homework.

PATRICK. A lifetime.

EDWARD. Your point?

PATRICK. And now. Just like that.

EDWARD. I've had enough.

PATRICK. So because of this one point, this issue –

EDWARD. Yes.

PATRICK. The homosexuals.

EDWARD. Not only.

PATRICK. Because of the gays, Edward.

EDWARD. Though it's reason enough.

PATRICK. Because of this one disagreement.

EDWARD. It's *emblematic*.

PATRICK. You're going to leave.

Pause.

EDWARD. I've never seen that sort of hatred. It beggars belief. I've tried hard to understand it but I can't. It has nothing to do with what I know of Christianity. It's irreconcilable.

PATRICK. We are fighting for the soul of Africa, Edward, you know it well. Christianity needs to prevail in its purest form. It is not the time for any sort of relativism. Moral certainties are necessary.

EDWARD. Nothing moral about them.

PATRICK. And so the Archbishop received your letter of resignation. He was upset, if not surprised.

EDWARD. Upset, was he?

PATRICK. Devastated.

EDWARD. That's more like it.

PATRICK. We want you to reconsider.

EDWARD. Do you now?

PATRICK. After all, you're a great asset.

EDWARD. An asset?

PATRICK. A crude word, I know, but I'm being blunt.

EDWARD. In what way am I an asset?

PATRICK. You have continuously challenged us with your many unorthodox opinions over the years, ranging in subject matter from the ordination of women bishops to ways of combating inner-city crime and the efforts to eradicate AIDS from sub-Saharan Africa.

EDWARD. Thank you for reminding me.

PATRICK. I think in that last example I mentioned you proposed the Italian Air Force bombarding Africa with condoms decorated with the face of the Pope.

EDWARD. Did I?

PATRICK. We all remember you chained to the railings of the Chinese Embassy.

EDWARD. Oh, that.

PATRICK. As well as the controversial piece you wrote in the *New Statesman* naming the three great Jewish prophets as Moses, Jesus Christ and Karl Marx.

EDWARD. That was good, wasn't it.

PATRICK. I suppose what I'm saying, Edward, is that everyone in the Church welcomes and actively appreciates your often uncomfortable, always exciting contribution to the larger theological debate.

EDWARD. I'm not sure all of your colleagues would agree.

PATRICK. Without voices like yours, the Church would slumber and stagnate.

EDWARD. Instead, it's right out there on the cutting edge.

PATRICK. We *need* you is what I'm saying.

EDWARD. Is that the best you can do?

PATRICK. The night is young.

Slight pause.

EDWARD. I hate to be the bearer of bad news but you're at a disadvantage.

PATRICK. I am?

EDWARD. Your timing is unfortunate, my daughter is here.

PATRICK. Sophie?

EDWARD. With an American. A *New Yorker*, he keeps correcting me. An aspiring novelist. They were working on a production of *Hamlet* together in Cornwall. I think it's love.

PATRICK. I look forward to seeing her, it's been years.

EDWARD. But there's a problem.

PATRICK. And the problem is?

EDWARD. I haven't told her yet.

PATRICK. Told her…?

EDWARD. That I'm resigning. That as of tomorrow morning I am no longer bishop of anywhere. That I'm a layman, a recluse, a defeated old man.

PATRICK. You've been deceitful, Edward?

EDWARD. I'm picking my moment, that's all.

PATRICK. And the moment is?

EDWARD. Tomorrow morning. At the port. As she's boarding the ferry.

PATRICK. And the reason…?

EDWARD. She's obdurate and determined like you.

PATRICK. And she'll try to dissuade you.

EDWARD. So tonight is our last night together. Please don't spoil it.

PATRICK. You're putting me in a very difficult situation.

EDWARD. I don't recall sending you an invitation to dinner.

PATRICK. You're asking me to lie.

EDWARD. I'm asking you to respect my wishes in my house.

PATRICK. And lie.

EDWARD. And wait until tomorrow morning.

PATRICK. At the port. When we're boarding the ferry.

EDWARD. That is correct.

PATRICK. I… Edward… I…

EDWARD. So let's be civil and respect each other's needs.

SOPHIE and TOM *enter from the house.*

SOPHIE. Oh. My. God.

EDWARD. Sophie, you remember Patrick?

SOPHIE. Remember him!

She runs up to him and they embrace.

PATRICK. Hello, Sophie.

SOPHIE. This is the man I was telling you about.

PATRICK. You were talking about me?

SOPHIE. The other day. I was telling Tom about this young priest who taught me children's songs in Swahili.

PATRICK. Young, yes.

EDWARD. And now he's old and a bishop.

SOPHIE. Patrick, this is Tom.

TOM. I'm from New York.

SOPHIE. What are you... (*To* EDWARD.) You didn't say... I mean, that you were coming.

PATRICK. No.

SOPHIE. I mean, this is –

TOM. It's great to meet you, sir.

SOPHIE. Fantastic, yes, but why didn't you say?

EDWARD. Because I didn't know.

SOPHIE. But what brought you here?

   Pause.

PATRICK. Well, I...

EDWARD. He's passing through.

PATRICK. Edward.

SOPHIE. It's a seven-hour ferry trip from Athens.

EDWARD. He's come to ask me something. It's work-related.

SOPHIE. Work-related?

EDWARD. Things, you know.

TOM. Church things.

EDWARD. Yes, thank you, Tom, Church things.

SOPHIE. All this way? Why didn't you call.

TOM. Things to do with Jesus and things.

PATRICK. I have come to make an urgent request of your father.

SOPHIE. Concerning?

26

EDWARD. It's private.

SOPHIE. Nothing serious?

EDWARD. No, nothing serious.

PATRICK. Quite serious, yes.

EDWARD. Serious to us, but not to you.

PATRICK. That's not quite true.

SOPHIE. This is all a bit strange.

EDWARD. Nothing strange about it at all. And now, if you don't mind. I will escort Patrick to his room so that he can leave his bag and freshen up or whatever he has to do and then we will all convene here on this terrace with this view of the Aegean to enjoy dinner and discuss various topics, preferably all trivial.

TOM. That sounds cool.

EDWARD. Patrick, follow me.

He walks off with PATRICK *in tow.*

TOM. Jesus, that is so weird.

SOPHIE. What is?

TOM. I've never met a bishop in my life and then I meet two in three days.

SOPHIE. They often hang out with each other.

He walks up to her, puts his arms around her.

TOM. Okay, so you ready?

SOPHIE. No.

TOM. Sophie, you need to do it.

SOPHIE. I don't want to.

TOM. Jesus, you must think he really hates me.

SOPHIE. It's not that.

TOM. Is it the 'living in sin' thing?

SOPHIE. I told you, he's cool.

TOM. A cool bishop.

SOPHIE. If he knows we love each other.

TOM. Then what?

SOPHIE. I'll tell him tomorrow.

TOM. *Tomorrow?*

SOPHIE. Before we get on the boat.

TOM *pulls away.*

TOM. Okay, you know what, this is not good, I mean, are you ashamed of me?

SOPHIE. You know I'm not.

TOM. Because, Jesus, I'm beginning to take this personally.

SOPHIE. He doesn't know you.

TOM. That's why we came here. So that he could meet me.

SOPHIE. It's three days.

TOM. Enough time for him to establish that I don't kill babies.

SOPHIE. I'm his only... the only person he has.

TOM. He's a bishop, he has his flock or whatever it's called, his... his herd.

SOPHIE. I'll take him aside tomorrow morning.

TOM. All you're doing is putting it off.

SOPHIE. Or maybe, I don't know –

TOM. If he needs references he can write to my parents. Well, maybe not my dad but my mother definitely. I love you. You love me. You are moving to New York and we are going to try the cohabitation thing. I will do this advertising gig –

SOPHIE. While you're working on your next draft.

TOM. So that we can have some money coming in and you can apply for the journalism course and I will help you and support you and be a good hunter-gatherer and we will be happy and perhaps one day bring forth new life onto this planet.

SOPHIE. You're scaring me.

TOM. So I am going to tell him tonight.

SOPHIE. No. I mean, I will. Please. Let me. I promise.

TATYANA *walks on with another tray laden with more plates and glasses for the table, muttering in Russian as she does so.*

TATYANA. Я даже слушать его не должна; надо делать так, как я считаю нужным. [*Pronounced: 'Ja dazhe slushat evo ne dolzhna; nado delat' tak, kak ja cshitau nuzhnum.' Meaning: 'I shouldn't even listen to him, I should do what I know is right.'*]

SOPHIE. Do you need some help, Tatyana?

TATYANA. There is not enough food for everyone but it is not my fault, I said to him we need more.

SOPHIE. We'll manage.

TATYANA. And now he bring the black man.

SOPHIE. His name is Patrick, he's from Kenya.

TATYANA. Where are they?

SOPHIE. He's just showing him to his room. They'll be down in a minute.

TATYANA *checks to make sure they can't be heard.*

TATYANA. Sophia.

SOPHIE. Tatyana.

TATYANA. Your father has the screw loose.

SOPHIE. And it's taken you this long to find out?

TATYANA. He forget everything. This morning I think he eat the smokey salmon. This is fine, I have no problem, he can eat it all, I don't care.

SOPHIE. So?

TATYANA. So now I say, 'Edward, did you eat the smokey salmon?' and he says, 'No, I did not eat the smokey salmon.'

TOM. But you don't believe him.

TATYANA. I don't think he is lying, why should he be lying, I think he forgets.

SOPHIE. Well, that happens.

TATYANA. But every day, twenty things like this.

SOPHIE. Maybe you're exaggerating.

TATYANA. And then he is so angry. And now, since we come from England, even more angry, very angry.

SOPHIE. He has his reasons.

TOM. It's to do with the gays.

TATYANA. He is angry with the gays?

SOPHIE. No, it's the opposite, but yes, he's angry.

TATYANA. Every day losing the temper, shouting, из всего устраивает сцену. [*Pronounced: 'iz vsevo us-tra-i-va-jet stzsenu.' Meaning: 'making a scene about everything.'*]

TOM. Maybe we should tell him tomorrow after all.

TATYANA. I say to him, 'Why are you angry, Edward, why always shouting?' He says to me something like, 'I am shouting against the closing of the light.'

SOPHIE. Raging, yes.

TATYANA. Maybe it is better now that we are not going back to England. That we are staying. Maybe he relaxes.

SOPHIE. What do you mean not going back?

TATYANA. And he is right to be angry with the gays. They are funny sometimes but dangerous too.

She leaves.

TOM. Okay. That's interesting. She's articulated what I've always felt. They *are* dangerous. I have this theory that they want to take over the world and force us all to subscribe to *The World of Interiors*. I'll talk to her about it.

SOPHIE. What did she mean, they're not going back to England?

EDWARD *and* PATRICK *return.*

EDWARD. So, yes, good, that's all sorted.

PATRICK. Now I see why you keep coming back to this place.

EDWARD. Sophie's mother bought it in the late seventies for a few thousand drachma.

SOPHIE. It was one of the last things she did.

PATRICK. A refuge.

TOM. No wonder it means so much to you.

SOPHIE. Dad, Tatyana just said something about you not going back to England.

EDWARD. Confused, as ever.

During the next few lines, EDWARD *pours* TOM *and* SOPHIE *a couple of ouzos and tops up his own.*

PATRICK. So, young man, Edward tells me you have just been involved in a production of *Hamlet*.

SOPHIE. In Cornwall, yes.

TOM. We both were. Sophie was playing Ophelia and I was assisting her.

EDWARD. I'm sure you were.

SOPHIE. He was the assistant director is what he means.

PATRICK. How interesting.

TOM. It's not what I had in mind when I decided to come to Europe for the summer.

PATRICK. An extended holiday?

TOM. Following my postgrad course, yes.

PATRICK. And prior to?

TOM. Moving back to the city. And a temporary job.

EDWARD. You never said what the job was.

TOM. Oh, it's just temporary.

SOPHIE. Tom is a writer.

TOM. Something to keep me going. A good cash job.

EDWARD. Doing what?

SOPHIE. What he really wants to do is write.

PATRICK. Well, good luck to you.

They've all settled in various points around the space, some sitting, some standing.

EDWARD. So what's *Hamlet* about, Tom?

TOM. What's *Hamlet* about?

EDWARD. In a word.

SOPHIE. He does this.

TOM. Well, let's see, I suppose –

EDWARD. Instinctively.

TOM. A call to arms?

EDWARD. Against?

TOM. Something spurious, I suppose, unreal.

EDWARD. I agree.

TOM. As well as the usurpation of power by the undeserving.

SOPHIE. The morally corrupt.

PATRICK. Something rotten.

TOM. Exactly.

EDWARD. And do you relate at all, *connect*, Tom? To Hamlet, I mean?

TOM. Doesn't everyone?

EDWARD. I'm not interested in everyone, I'm interested in you.

SOPHIE. Why the inquisition all of a sudden?

EDWARD. Oh, I'm sorry, I didn't mean to –

TOM. It's fine, really, I'm enjoying this.

EDWARD. It's just I don't really know you. I mean, you've been here for three days but all I really know is that you eat very quickly and have a penchant for psychedelic swimming trunks… But the *measure* of the man.

TOM. Of course I relate to Hamlet. I can't see how it would be possible not to.

EDWARD. In what way do you relate to him?

TOM. His procrastinations, anxieties, weaknesses.

EDWARD. And what about his calling?

TOM. His calling?

EDWARD. 'A call to arms,' you said. I'm assuming you meant it was Hamlet who was being called?

TOM. Oh, that.

EDWARD. And do you have a calling?

SOPHIE. He's a writer.

TOM. Well, maybe not as pronounced as yours.

EDWARD. What do you know of my calling?

TOM. No, I mean, what I mean is I haven't been called in that way, I mean, I'm not a bishop –

SOPHIE. Now you tell me.

TOM. I haven't a *religious* calling is what I mean, I haven't been blessed in that way.

EDWARD. Oh, it's a blessing, is it?

TOM. But yes, I suppose I have a calling –

EDWARD. Against the spurious, the unreal.

TOM. Doesn't everyone?

EDWARD. No, I don't think everyone does, but I assume that if I am to believe my daughter when she says that you are a writer of some importance –

SOPHIE. He is.

EDWARD. Well then, yes, I imagine that it is likely that you do have a calling. And it doesn't have to be religious.

PATRICK. Doesn't it?

EDWARD. You can choose your own word for it. For the time being let's hope it is a calling towards a state more truthful than the one we currently find ourselves in.

TOM. Okay.

EDWARD. And you are a procrastinator?

TOM. Well, I –

EDWARD. Because you said that's one of the characteristics that you share with Hamlet. It was the first word you used.

TOM. I, sometimes, yes, perhaps, I think –

EDWARD. You lack conviction?

TOM. It is harder for some of us to know what we believe. I envy the certainties of the religious-minded, that's for sure.

EDWARD. Yes, I envy Patrick too, but for the less literal-minded of us, certainty is a luxury we can't afford.

PATRICK. Edward, Edward, Edward.

EDWARD. Certainty is a state of mind, faith is a state of heart. There's a marked difference, I believe.

SOPHIE. What's got into you?

PATRICK. Edward, you're inviting a response.

EDWARD. I'm just trying to get to know the man.

SOPHIE. In a very weird manner.

EDWARD. But I'm sorry if it's coming across the wrong way.

TOM. It's cool.

EDWARD. Just getting to know you.

SOPHIE. Is that what it's called?

TATYANA *comes in with the last of the dishes and some serving spoons.*

EDWARD. At last, I thought you were trying to starve us.

TATYANA. It isn't very much but is ready anyway.

SOPHIE. There's loads.

TATYANA. Меня вы, конечно, никогда не слушаете.
[*Pronounced: 'Menia vu kone-shno ni-kag-da ne-slu-sha-e-te.'*
Meaning: 'But you never listen to me, of course.']

EDWARD. Well, help yourselves.

For the next few minutes they all help themselves to some of the food and then sit in various places around the table. It's all very casual.

PATRICK. This is a veritable feast.

TATYANA. I tell you there is not enough.

SOPHIE. This looks beautiful, Tatyana.

TATYANA. You are welcome.

They continue to serve themselves from the dishes. EDWARD *bows his head to say grace, the rest follow suit with* TOM *doing a bit of an awkward imitation.*

EDWARD. Bless oh Lord this food for our use and make us ever mindful of the needs of others. Amen.

PATRICK. Amen.

TOM. Absolutely.

They all tuck in.

But you know it's interesting, continuing in this vein of 'getting to know each other' –

EDWARD. Yes, let's.

TOM. Well, you know, I've never really met a bishop before, let alone two, and it's an amazing thing –

EDWARD. What is?

TOM. Because you know I suppose I don't come from any sort of religious background at all, I mean, my parents were very relaxed about that kind of thing, I mean, the most religious thing they ever did was baptise our Labrador but that was a kind of joke.

PATRICK. A joke?

SOPHIE. His parents were hippies, there were drugs involved.

TOM. But anyway, when I see you guys, I mean, even like now and you're not even wearing your purple robes, isn't that what you wear, purple things, what are they called, the bishop's habit, is it like a nun, do you say bishop's habit?

SOPHIE. Cassock.

TOM. The bishop's cassock, thank you, Sophie, and I mean when I see that and think of what you do for a living, and I mean I respect it, I really respect it, so this is not being said in a mocking or derogatory way at all –

SOPHIE. Tom-Tom.

TOM. But when I see that, what you guys do, what you are, I'm thinking this is so like *Mary Poppins*. Or *Bedknobs and Broomsticks*. That kind of thing.

No response.

What I'm saying is I'm sure it's an important, admirable thing, I mean, the Church and everything you guys are doing, is very important, I mean, really, but I suppose what I'm asking is, because maybe what I'm doing is asking a question here, that's part of what I'm doing, but what I'm really doing is asking really how it's possible in this day and age, for instance, you know after we've landed on the Moon and after Darwin and DNA and God knows what else, how it is possible to believe, for instance, that somebody a few thousand years ago turned water into wine and stuff like that and then actually was, not resuscitated, what's the word –

SOPHIE. Resurrected.

TOM. Resurrected, thank you, how it is possible to actually believe that, after, as I was saying, Galileo and Darwin and –

EDWARD. DNA, *yes*.

TOM. How that is possible.

Pause.

Unless you live in South Carolina.

Pause.

But I'm asking with respect.

Pause.

PATRICK. *Bedknobs and Broomsticks*, eh?

EDWARD. It's a valid question, Thomas. Let me think about it.

TOM. Cool.

They have all sat down by this point and are eating their dinner.

PATRICK. This is delicious, Tatyana.

TOM. It really is, it really is delicious. This thing you've done with the beets.

TATYANA. It is Russian.

TOM. I thought so, it has a kind of Slavic thing going on.

TATYANA. I am Russian.

PATRICK. Yes.

TATYANA. But from the Ukraine. Украина. [*Pronounced: 'Uk-ra-i-na.' Meaning: 'Ukraine.'*] A small town near Kiev called Horenka.

TOM. Well, they certainly know what to do with beets in Horenka.

Pause.

PATRICK. And how did the two of you meet, Edward?

TATYANA. Seven years ago. In Thessaloniki.

EDWARD. On my way to Mount Athos.

PATRICK. How interesting. And what brought you to Greece, Tatyana?

TATYANA. Prostitution.

PATRICK. I see.

Pause. They keep eating.

The potatoes are delicious too.

TOM. Yes, they're pleasantly moist.

Pause.

TATYANA. I am not ashamed to say. I did not choose that. I come with men who обещали [*Pronounced: 'o-be-csha-li' Meaning: 'promised'*] promise me work. I need to send money to my family. I thought maybe cleaning houses, looking after small children. But the men lie. Then one night, Edward pick me up in his car.

TOM. Kerb-crawling, Edward?

TATYANA. He take me back to his hotel. But no sex.

EDWARD. Alas, no.

TATYANA. No, talk, talk, talk, as always. He ask me if I enjoy the work.

EDWARD. Not quite the way I phrased it.

TOM. And you said…

TATYANA. You think I enjoy all the ugly men putting their things in me?

PATRICK. That can't be nice.

TATYANA. So, he says, 'I live in England, I will help you out with papers so you can come to the UK,' and he says, 'I also have a house on Patmos, in Greece and you look after me, I am an old man, maybe cooking and things' –

PATRICK. And that's what happened.

TATYANA. I ask him, 'Will you put your thing in me too, Edward?'

EDWARD. She did.

TOM. It's good to be direct.

TATYANA. And he says, I have not forgotten because I look up in the lexicon, the dictionary, he says, 'No, I will refrain from putting my thing in you.'

SOPHIE. That's a relief.

TATYANA. And is true, he refrain. But he is difficult man.

TOM. Very. I mean, yes, well, aren't we all in different ways.

Pause.

EDWARD. When I met Tatyana, she had an air of bewilderment about her.

TATYANA. What is this?

SOPHIE. It means like you were surprised, caught off-guard.

PATRICK. By what?

EDWARD. A bewilderment at finding herself in a country she hardly knew, trying to communicate in a language she didn't speak, doing a job she hadn't chosen, living a life she wasn't expecting –

TATYANA. It's true.

EDWARD. All decided for her by these men whose sole purpose was to accumulate more and more money at her expense.

TATYANA. I remember, Edward.

EDWARD. And so she was bewildered. And so am I.

Pause. They continue to pick at their food.

You two are going to miss each other, aren't you?

SOPHIE. We are.

EDWARD. Not that you can't go over from time to time. Holidays, that sort of thing.

TOM. We were going to talk to you about that.

SOPHIE. *In the morning.*

EDWARD. Talk to me about what?

TOM. About the fact that Sophie's moving to New York. To be. With me. In a couple of weeks. Sir.

Pause.

EDWARD. Well.

SOPHIE. It's true. For a little time. I mean, just for a while, Dad. And then we'll see.

TOM. There's this course at Columbia.

EDWARD. So it's more than just a summer romance.

TOM. Well, we certainly hope so.

SOPHIE. Just for a little time.

TOM. And then maybe for ever.

SOPHIE. But really I'm just going over to stay for a year or so. And then we'll see.

Pause.

EDWARD. What can I say? Big changes.

SOPHIE. Yes.

EDWARD. Congratulations.

TOM. Thank you.

EDWARD. So.

SOPHIE. Yes.

EDWARD. Congratulations. A toast. To change. New things. New days.

PATRICK. New days.

TOM. Yes. New days.

They toast.

SOPHIE. I wanted… I was going… to talk to you about it.

EDWARD. Were you?

SOPHIE. I didn't mean to tell you like this.

EDWARD. Of course not.

TOM. We just thought it best –

SOPHIE. So suddenly, I mean.

TOM. I think Sophie was a little nervous of telling you.

EDWARD. Whatever for? You love each other. You're moving to New York.

SOPHIE. For a few months anyway.

TOM. But you must come and visit.

EDWARD. I hate New York.

TOM. I'm sorry.

EDWARD. But congratulations.

A long, awkward pause. TOM *attempts a new subject with forced enthusiasm.*

TOM. So, the gay question.

EDWARD. What about it?

TOM. I was wondering if we could talk about it.

SOPHIE. Do we have to?

TATYANA. What is the gay question?

TOM. I just thought it would be interesting, seeing as it's such a hot topic, I mean, isn't that what you were all arguing about in… what's that place –

SOPHIE. Lambeth.

TOM. At the Lambeth conference of bishops and priests and I'm just wondering what the whole deal was about.

Pause.

In that 'getting to know each other' kind of way.

Pause.

EDWARD. All right then, Patrick, why don't you tell Tom what happened in Lambeth.

PATRICK. Why don't you?

EDWARD. Because history is written by the winners.

PATRICK. Oh, Edward.

TOM. But I really am very interested.

Pause. PATRICK *takes a moment before beginning.*

PATRICK. Let's see. Well, Tom, resolutions were passed that enforce the Church's commitment to helping support people of homosexual orientation –

EDWARD. As long as they're not homosexual.

PATRICK. Through pastoral care and God's transformative power –

EDWARD. Converting gays into straights with the power of prayer is what he means.

PATRICK. But ultimately affirming that homosexual practice is incompatible with Scripture –

EDWARD. Along with eating shellfish.

PATRICK. As is sexual promiscuity in all its forms –

EDWARD. Whilst paradoxically refusing to legitimise or give blessing to same-sex unions.

TOM. Jeez, it must have been a pretty busy conference. All those decisions made.

PATRICK. It wasn't easy.

EDWARD. The thing you need to understand, Tom, is that Patrick and many men like him just wish homosexuality didn't exist. Somewhere along the line he's confused what he doesn't like the idea of aesthetically with what is morally right or wrong.

PATRICK. Please don't speak for me, Edward.

EDWARD. Either that or he's just concerned about the dwindling global population.

SOPHIE. And a surplus of natural resources.

EDWARD. Along with this distaste of anything to do with matters anal, he also finds himself intimidated by any sort of ambiguity.

PATRICK. I do?

EDWARD. It is a known fact that the covert fascist in everyone appreciates clearly defined categories, not those murky shades in between.

PATRICK. You're calling me a fascist, Edward?

EDWARD. You will find, Patrick, that that particular characteristic is shared with the more militant European racist to whom the idea of a mixed-race child is an appalling aberration. Black and white with nothing in between.

PATRICK. That's a profoundly offensive comparison.

EDWARD. Straight men and straight women with nothing in between.

SOPHIE. Why are you being so aggressive?

EDWARD. Of course, here in Greece a few thousand years before Freud and Kinsey, Plato was already referring to the third sex which existed somewhere between the other two.

TATYANA. Like the transvestites.

EDWARD. So it is interesting to consider that if we'd inherited our morals from the Greek instead of the Hebrew tradition, Patrick could well be citing him to explain his passionate support for gay and lesbian rights.

PATRICK. As you can see, Edward feels strongly on the subject.

EDWARD. But then using scapegoats is the oldest trick in the book. The gays come in handy from time to time, don't they, Patrick?

PATRICK. Please, Edward.

EDWARD. So instead of worrying about the fact the world is riddled with corruption, horrific inequalities, random brutality and a criminal lack of education, let us decide to spend most of our energies condemning people who are only seeking a blessing for their loving relationships. This is what is left of Christianity.

He stands, his tone increasing in intensity over the next few minutes.

Go on then, Patrick. Tell them why you're here and then I'll answer Tom's question on what made me choose this particular path in life.

SOPHIE. What's he talking about, Patrick?

TATYANA. Why you stand up, Edward? Sit down and finish eating.

EDWARD. Tell Sophie why you're here.

PATRICK. Shouldn't you do that?

EDWARD. Patrick made this diversion on his way home in the futile hope of dissuading me from leaving the Church.

SOPHIE. Leaving the Church?

EDWARD. That's right.

SOPHIE. What are you talking about?

EDWARD. I told him, of course, that it's too late. That I'm already in exile.

SOPHIE. In exile?

EDWARD. In exile from a Church that is too busy reading the small print to hear anything of the meaning being imparted. A Church led by spiritual bureaucrats and their literalist lackeys.

SOPHIE. What d'you mean, you're in exile?

EDWARD. A Church intent only in maintaining its own warped version of social control.

TATYANA. Why you getting angry, Edward?

EDWARD. Whilst sacrificing the true tenets of the Christian message.

SOPHIE. Dad.

EDWARD. So let's talk about bedknobs and broomsticks, Tom.

TOM. That didn't come out right.

EDWARD. It came out just fine.

SOPHIE. Why aren't you answering my question?

EDWARD. Let me tell you why I gave my life – FORTY-SEVEN YEARS of my life to stories of virgin births, prodigal sons and healed lepers. First, I love a good fucking metaphor. Nothing quite like it to elucidate and inspire. Secondly, I fell madly, passionately – yes, Tom, *irrationally* – in love with another man.

TATYANA. You are a gay, Edward?

EDWARD. Don't worry, Patrick, bodily fluids were not exchanged and the anal passage was left untouched.

SOPHIE. What are you talking about?

EDWARD. A man who seemed at least to me to speak of love as the most subversive power in the world. The only power able to combat the innate greed and selfishness which now seems to be destroying everything around us.

TATYANA. Oh, he means Jesus, thank God.

EDWARD. The only power that can remind us that the markets are there to serve us and not the other fucking way around. That there is more to life than the lowest common denominator.

Pause.

That is why I gave my life to bedknobs and broomsticks, Tom. Not to perpetuate primitive prejudice. I hope that answers your question.

TOM. Emphatically.

Pause. They have all been taken aback by EDWARD's *outburst.*

TATYANA. My nephew in the Ukraine, I think he is gay. On his wall, two thousand pictures of Britney Spears.

EDWARD. Nietzsche was only part right. Your God is dead, Patrick. But not God. God changes with us, that's all.

PATRICK *stands, moves towards the house, then stops and turns to* EDWARD.

PATRICK. I've outstayed my welcome. Tatyana, thank you for the delicious food.

TATYANA. There was not enough.

PATRICK. There are some rooms on the harbour, they seemed nice enough. I'll stay there for the night.

EDWARD. Don't be a fool.

SOPHIE. Patrick.

PATRICK. The one thing we now agree on, Edward, is that my coming here was in vain. A few minutes ago I was praising your maverick spirit. But I fear that your arguments have now become more personal and just a little uglier.

EDWARD. I've been provoked.

PATRICK. You seem to think that you can impose your views on the rest of the world with scant consideration of the needs of different societies and a complete disrespect of their cultures. Some would call this attitude colonial and just a little arrogant. Old habits die hard, I see.

EDWARD. I'm running out of time.

PATRICK. Let us not forget, by the way, that fifty years ago you Brits were busy importing your own particular brand of homophobia to my country along with scones and strawberry jam.

EDWARD. That wasn't me.

PATRICK. Now, all of a sudden you've changed your minds.

EDWARD. It's called progress.

PATRICK. Oh, is that what it is?

Pause.

Forgive me, but to me, it appears different. From where I stand it seems like yet another manifestation of a society that has lost its moral compass at the altar of personal entitlement. I love the sinner as much as you do, Edward, you know that. But I will not be seduced into loving the sin.

EDWARD. The only sin is the absence of love.

PATRICK. The combination of your naivety and idealism is a dangerous one. You fail to understand what we need for the Church to survive is for moderation and gradualism. If we followed your ways in Africa, within a few years the Anglican Church would be dead and Islam would reign supreme. And where would that leave the gays, I wonder.

Pause.

Perhaps I was wrong. Perhaps it is right that you are leaving the Church, Edward. Perhaps it is time.

A pause and then PATRICK *enters the house.*

EDWARD. Don't let him go. Tell him to stay.

SOPHIE. I'll try.

She runs after him into the house. TATYANA *starts to clear the dishes.*

TATYANA. Why you always angry, Edward, why you shouting. You need to rest. No more screaming against the switching off of the light. Ты уже пожилой человек, тебе надо отдыхать. [*Pronounced: 'Tee oo-zheh pah-zhee-loy tcheh-lah-vyek, tee-byeh nah-da aht-dee-khat.' Meaning: 'You are an old man now, you need to rest.'*]

She walks off to the kitchen carrying a tray of dishes.

EDWARD *and* TOM *are left alone. There is a pause.* EDWARD *is looking out, towards the sea.*

EDWARD. This is the time of day. The sky.

TOM. It's beautiful.

Pause.

EDWARD. What's your novel called?

TOM. Working title: *The Missing Man.*

EDWARD. Sophie said it's important and urgent. Those were the words she chose.

TOM. She talks me up a little.

EDWARD. What's it about?

TOM. Okay, let's see. There's a hero. But he's this guy who kind of –

EDWARD. Procrastinates.

TOM. How did you know? And has this sort of –

EDWARD. Calling.

TOM. Towards a state more truthful than the one he finds himself in.

Pause.

It's mostly comic. And then tragic. Or the other way round.

Pause.

Are you really leaving the Church?

EDWARD *doesn't answer.*

EDWARD. Why do you want to be a writer, Tom?

TOM. You ask the easiest questions.

EDWARD. What compels you to write?

TOM. Things that I want to communicate.

EDWARD. Such as?

TOM. I am here. I feel this. I feel that. I hope this. I hope that.

EDWARD. Go on.

TOM. Do you feel this? Do you feel that? Do you hope this? Do you hope that?

EDWARD. Most probably.

TOM. And then…

EDWARD. I'm listening.

TOM. This is also possible.

EDWARD. Yes.

TOM. The way things are is not the only way. There's more. Something else.

EDWARD. I agree.

TOM. Which I can't quite rationally…

EDWARD. Grasp?

TOM. Not yet.

EDWARD. That's what I mean about loving a good metaphor. It's reaching for it.

TOM. Reaching.

EDWARD. That's who you are. Don't ever forget that.

Pause.

Stories.

TOM. What about them?

EDWARD. They're all we have.

TOM. Sure.

EDWARD. And the one I've given my life to is a good one. Even though many have done their best to warp it.

TOM. Yes.

EDWARD. But its time is up.

Pause.

Look after her.

Suddenly, he is overcome by an emotion but he restrains it.

Nihilism is the victory of the status quo, Tom.

TOM. Okay.

EDWARD. And so it's time for the storytellers again.

TOM. The storytellers?

EDWARD. The shamans. The real priests. The storytellers.

Their eyes meet. They stare at each other.

The storytellers, Tom.

Somewhere in the background, the sound of wings fluttering, a bird taking flight.

Blackout.

End of Act One.

ACT TWO

Scene One

2006

An afternoon in late summer in a large room in a country-house-type hotel, somewhere in England. The furniture has all been cleared and from the large doors towards the back of the room we can hear the sounds of a party in the next room – music, laughter, chatting, the clinking of glasses.

SOPHIE *hobbles in on one shoe, holding the other one in her hand, with* SEBASTIAN *following closely behind. Both are smartly dressed, both are holding glasses of something.*

SOPHIE. Shit, shit, shit.

SEBASTIAN. I'm not surprised.

SOPHIE. I need some glue.

SEBASTIAN. The way you were dancing.

SOPHIE. What about it?

SEBASTIAN. It was crazy.

SOPHIE. Is that a bad thing?

SEBASTIAN. It's just…

SOPHIE. Go on.

SEBASTIAN. Honestly? I have never known you drink this much, Sophie.

SOPHIE. Haven't you?

SEBASTIAN. Two mojitos, two champagnes before lunch –

SOPHIE. Oh my God, you're counting.

SEBASTIAN. And at least half a bottle of that Sauvignon Blanc.

SOPHIE. Where are you going with this?

SEBASTIAN. I'm just wondering if there's a reason.

SOPHIE. Sebastian, I got back just under a week ago.

SEBASTIAN. I know you did.

SOPHIE. I was there for three months.

SEBASTIAN. I know you were.

SOPHIE. During those three months I had a myriad of experiences. I spent time with a thirteen-year-old girl who'd watched her father's head being sawn off for trying to make a living as an interpreter. I walked around a marketplace after a bomb had been detonated leaving a sea of severed limbs in its wake, I'm now at a gay wedding in Surrey. I'm letting my hair down. Is that a good enough reason?

SEBASTIAN. The American.

SOPHIE. What American?

SEBASTIAN. It is strange that you haven't talked to him.

SOPHIE. Is it?

SEBASTIAN. I thought maybe he was the reason.

SOPHIE. That must be his girlfriend. The very thin woman.

SEBASTIAN. Won't you speak to each other?

SOPHIE. I'm sure we will at some point. And if we do, we do, and if we don't, we don't.

SEBASTIAN. I love you, Sophie.

Pause. She smiles.

Okay, here goes. Fuck. I am a little nervous, it's understandable.

SOPHIE. Nervous?

SEBASTIAN. I've never done this thing before.

SOPHIE. What thing?

SEBASTIAN. Maybe I should blame my mother. On the phone every day from Chile, driving me crazy.

SOPHIE. I'm not sure I understand.

SEBASTIAN. Or maybe it's just because we're here. I've been inspired.

SOPHIE. Sebastian, what are you talking about?

SEBASTIAN. Funny to think I've always condemned marriage as a bourgeois convention.

SOPHIE. Have you?

SEBASTIAN. And I know we haven't been together for such a long time but sometimes you have to be bold and –

SOPHIE. Sebastian.

SEBASTIAN. Sophie.

SOPHIE. Glue.

SEBASTIAN. Glue?

SOPHIE. I need some glue. I feel at a disadvantage. Temporarily disabled, that sort of thing.

Pause.

Please find me some glue, something. And then we can... you can... but in the meantime I'm in desperate need of some glue.

SEBASTIAN. Yes. Glue.

He makes a move to go. LAWRENCE bursts in, rummaging through his pockets as he does so. He is dressed to the nines. He is in a state of panic.

LAWRENCE. Calamity, calamity, calamity. Appalling, horrendous calamity.

SOPHIE. What's wrong?

LAWRENCE. I've lost the speech, I've lost the speech, I've lost the speech.

SOPHIE. You've lost the speech?

LAWRENCE. I'd put it into my inside pocket this morning. But then I took the jacket off in that awful café where we had the fried eggs and it must have slipped out.

SOPHIE. Surely you remember it? I mean, it is the most important speech of your life.

LAWRENCE. I'd written it down, why would I memorise it? I was going to read it.

SEBASTIAN. Did you call the café?

LAWRENCE. Luke is doing that now. What's wrong with you? You're lopsided.

SOPHIE. My heel broke. Don't panic. We'll write it again.

LAWRENCE. It's a catastrophe.

SOPHIE. Sebastian was just going to get some glue. From reception. Can you ask them for a piece of paper and a pen as well?

LAWRENCE. I have a pen.

SEBASTIAN. Okay, I go.

SOPHIE. Thank you.

SEBASTIAN *rushes off*.

Breathe deeply. Maybe you should do some stretches or something.

LAWRENCE. Stretches?

SOPHIE. To relax, I mean.

LAWRENCE. Not the time for a fucking Pilates class, darling. This is a monumental crisis, up there with the Bay of Pigs.

SOPHIE. We'll write it again.

LAWRENCE. I feel sick.

Pause.

SOPHIE. I'm surprised Tom's here.

LAWRENCE. So am I.

SOPHIE. Why didn't you tell me, Lawrence?

LAWRENCE. I never thought he was going to come.

SOPHIE. But he's here.

LAWRENCE. All the way from New York, I mean. Why does it matter?

SOPHIE. Well, it doesn't. I mean, not a lot.

LAWRENCE. It's been five years. You're adults, you've moved on.

SOPHIE. Of course we have, I know that.

LAWRENCE. Unless, of course, you haven't.

SOPHIE. It's just I wish I was prepared.

LAWRENCE. In what way prepared? Armed with a chainsaw? Accompanied by a bullmastiff?

SOPHIE. These things are always awkward.

LAWRENCE. Anyway, darling, I hate to drag the spotlight off you but there are two hundred people waiting for me to make a brilliantly witty, unbearably moving speech and I have nothing to offer them other than an expression of absolute horror etched on my face.

SOPHIE. We'll write it together.

TOM and ANNIE walk in. TOM is holding a bottle of champagne in one hand and a glass in another. ANNIE is also holding a glass.

TOM. Jesus, Sophie.

SOPHIE. Hello, Tom.

LAWRENCE. Here he is.

SOPHIE. We were just talking about you.

LAWRENCE. In the kindest possible way.

SOPHIE. Yes, very kindly.

TOM. Sophie sweetie, this is Annie.

They both look at him.

I meant, Annie sweetie, this is Sophie.

LAWRENCE. A case of confused confectioneries.

ANNIE. I feel like I know you already.

SOPHIE. You do?

ANNIE. Tom has always said how wonderful you were as Ophelia. He said you were very convincing in the mad scenes.

TOM. Horatio was pretty damn hot as well.

LAWRENCE. The same, my lord, and your poor servant ever. That virginal Cornish summer.

TOM. Nothing virginal about it.

LAWRENCE. Speak for yourself. I was an un-plucked flower.

TOM. As far as I recall you were being plucked regularly.

SOPHIE. By Rosencrantz and Guildenstern, yes.

LAWRENCE. Don't bring up my sordid past, on this of all days.

SOPHIE. Good idea, let's not delve. What's done is done.

LAWRENCE. And here we are, just a little fatter, a little wiser.

SOPHIE. That's hopeful.

LAWRENCE. Cheers.

They toast.

And it was Rosencrantz and the Second Gravedigger.

SOPHIE *notices* ANNIE *staring at her.*

SOPHIE. It's my shoe. It's. The heel. It's broken.

She takes the other shoe off.

SEBASTIAN *runs in with glue in one hand and a piece of paper in the other.*

SEBASTIAN (*handing the glue to* SOPHIE *and the paper to* LAWRENCE). Glue for you, paper for you.

LAWRENCE. Thank you, thank you.

LAWRENCE *whips out his pen and gets to work.*

SOPHIE (*grabbing* SEBASTIAN *by the arm, digging her nails into him*). Darling, this is Tom and Annie.

SEBASTIAN. Hello, Tom, hello, Annie, I'm Sebastian.

TOM. Hi.

SEBASTIAN (*feeling her nails digging into him*). Ow.

SOPHIE. Sorry.

ANNIE. Hello, Sebastian.

LAWRENCE (*writing it down as he goes along*). *Ladies and gentlemen.*

SOPHIE. He's lost his speech. He has to write it again.

ANNIE. Oh, that's terrible.

LAWRENCE. *Ladies and gentlemen*. Then what?

SOPHIE. I didn't think you'd make it over.

TOM. It was the perfect excuse.

SEBASTIAN. Excuse?

TOM. To get on a plane. I miss it, is what I mean.

SEBASTIAN. You mean London?

TOM. And are you two, you know, married, or anything.

SOPHIE. No, not married, no.

TOM. Cool. I mean as in, who needs it, what I mean is, as long as you love each other, which obviously you do because otherwise you wouldn't be together, but marriage itself is overrated, I mean, it's just a piece of paper, it isn't really important…

LAWRENCE *throws him a look over his shoulder.*

… unless, of course, you're gay, in which case it is vital and significant because it is an essential validation of the love between. Two men. Or women. Because of the persecution, I mean. History of. Persecution.

ANNIE. We're engaged.

TOM. Yes, only just.

SOPHIE. Congratulations.

SEBASTIAN. Yes, congratulations.

SOPHIE (*beginning to work a little manically on the heel which she does over the next few lines*). If you'll excuse me, I need to apply myself.

TOM. I've been following your career by, the way.

SOPHIE. Is that what it's called?

TOM. That thing you wrote in *The Times* on the Indonesian sweatshops.

ANNIE. That was intense. Tom showed it to me.

LAWRENCE (*talking about his speech as he tries to remember it*). The resounding theme was undying love.

TOM. The letter you wrote to Donald Rumsfeld in *The New Republic*, that piece on Exxon Mobil.

SEBASTIAN. She has been busy making friends.

LAWRENCE. *Ladies and gentlemen.*

TOM. Lawrence said you just got back from Iraq.

SOPHIE. I did.

ANNIE. Oh my God, doing what?

SEBASTIAN. Examining the debris.

SOPHIE. Something for *Harper's*: 'After the Auction'. Is this the only glue they had?

SEBASTIAN. Investigating the consequences of imported freedom and democracy in the Middle East.

SOPHIE (*still struggling with the shoe and glue*). And doing interviews with the people on the ground as well.

SEBASTIAN. To use an American expression, Tom, the 'collateral damage' people.

LAWRENCE. *This is going to be short and far from sweet.*

TOM. I didn't actually coin that phrase myself, Sebastian.

SOPHIE. Not just the players, but the played.

ANNIE. The played?

LAWRENCE. It's coming back, it's coming back, it's coming back.

TOM. Well, I can't say I'm surprised. I always knew you were going to be more *Harper's* than *Harper's Bazaar*.

LAWRENCE (*writing away*). Oh my God, it's coming back.

SEBASTIAN. Sophie says you are a funny man.

TOM. How comforting to know that.

SEBASTIAN. You have a sense of humour?

TOM. I couldn't possibly say.

SEBASTIAN. Well, make the most of it. Laughing at everything is one of the luxuries of being privileged.

TOM. You never laugh, Sebastian?

LAWRENCE (*writing as he remembers*). *Jardin du Luxembourg…*

SEBASTIAN. I laugh at things that are funny, yes. But not as a means of distraction.

TOM. Sebastian, take it easy, we've only just met.

SOPHIE (*still struggling with the heel*). Sebastian's been angry lately. Oh, and he's a Marxist.

ANNIE. I *love* Europe.

SEBASTIAN. I'm from Chile.

ANNIE. Oh, I'm sorry.

TOM. Does that pay well these days?

SEBASTIAN. I teach.

TOM. Twentieth-century history?

SEBASTIAN. Political theory at UCL.

TOM. Is it difficult trying to be objective?

SOPHIE. This glue really isn't working.

SEBASTIAN. I just try and remind my students that the successful politician, like the successful economist, is the one that convinces the world that his way is the only option.

ANNIE. That makes sense.

SEBASTIAN. And that my students' job is to prove them wrong.

TOM. Good luck to you.

SEBASTIAN. I suppose I am inviting them to exercise their wills and minds in unexpected ways. To surprise themselves and never give up.

ANNIE. That's admirable.

SEBASTIAN. And you are in advertising, Tom?

SOPHIE. Only temporarily. This isn't going to work. We need some of that industrial-strength stuff.

SEBASTIAN. It's the only one they had.

SOPHIE (*sits on the floor to continue working on the broken heel*). Excuse me, don't mind me, I really need to focus on this.

SEBASTIAN. And what do you do, Annie?

ANNIE. I'm an interior decorator.

TOM. One of the best in New York.

SEBASTIAN. That's great.

SOPHIE (*focused on the shoe*). I love a good sofa.

ANNIE. I design houses for rich people.

SOPHIE. Lucky you. This really isn't working.

SEBASTIAN. Movie stars and things?

ANNIE. A few.

TOM. She's very successful.

SOPHIE. Ship owners, bankers?

ANNIE. That kind of thing.

SOPHIE. Arms dealers?

ANNIE. You two haven't seen each other since…?

TOM. Not in five years.

SOPHIE. It's the 11th on Tuesday.

LAWRENCE. You were right, it's all coming back to me. Okay, here goes, listen and then chip in if you remember any other bits.

SOPHIE. We're all ears.

LAWRENCE (*reading*). 'Ladies and gentlemen.

TOM. It's good to start with something familiar.

LAWRENCE. I wish I could say I met Luke in the Jardin du Luxembourg on an autumnal evening –

ANNIE. I love the Jardin du Luxembourg.

LAWRENCE. – or even in the Cotswolds at Christmas. Fact is I met him at a bar called Fist in Croydon. It was love at first sight even though we couldn't actually see each other. But when he took off his mask, I was smitten. Relax, Mother, I'm joking. It was at the Costa Coffee on Old Compton Street and we were wearing Zara.' That's all I remember.

SOPHIE. There was something about opposites. The attraction of opposites.

LAWRENCE. Genius, you're a genius.

He resumes with the paper and pen.

ANNIE. Do you remember we spent that afternoon in the Jardin du Luxembourg when we were in Paris, sweetie? Just sitting on that bench with our books.

SOPHIE. I'll always associate you with that day, Tom.

TOM. Which part of it exactly?

ANNIE. Which day?

SOPHIE. Maybe just because it was the last time we saw each other. Before I moved out –

TOM. The falling buildings, the jumping people or the sky on fire?

SOPHIE. – and then came back here.

TOM. Or just the general catastrophe?

SEBASTIAN. Oh, that day.

SOPHIE. Isn't it funny how there are days that come along every so often, these events, these things that happen that are like these big signposts saying –

ANNIE. Signposts?

TOM. Saying what?

SOPHIE. Okay, this isn't going to work. Fuck it, I'm going barefoot.

She tosses her shoes away. Stands up. She takes the bottle of champagne from TOM.

May I?

She pours herself a glass.

Anyone else?

ANNIE. Saying what?

SOPHIE. Saying: 'Stop! Stop where you are! Stop right there! Cease being what you are for just one minute and reflect a little, pause for just one millisecond before you simply *react in haste*

and instead ask yourself in all honesty the imperative questions:
"How did I get here? Where am I headed? Why has this
happened?"' Don't you think, Annie?

Pause.

Anyone else for a drink?

SEBASTIAN. No, thank you.

TOM. I'll have a little.

She pours him some.

ANNIE. Truthfully? I think people are jealous of us, that's all. In the
West, I mean.

SOPHIE. Is that what it is?

SEBASTIAN. I think that's a little reductive.

LAWRENCE. I don't like where this conversation is headed.

ANNIE. And, you know, to be honest, I have to take issue with
where you're going with this because you know I'm a liberal,
and open-minded and yes, let's be aware of the bigger picture
and all that, but there are certain things which are never
justified –

SOPHIE. I don't think that's what I'm doing.

LAWRENCE. Can you go back to talking about sofas, please?

ANNIE. Acts of the most appalling barbarity and evil and when we
start justifying –

SEBASTIAN. Who is justifying anything?

ANNIE. When we start *justifying* certain things then we're in
trouble and maybe it's because I'm closer to the whole thing, I
mean, apart from being a New Yorker –

LAWRENCE. Or fabrics, or swatches?

ANNIE. Apart from that, maybe it has something to do with the fact
that I lost someone. A friend. Because I had a friend who died in
the North Tower. Sandy. So maybe that's why I feel quite
strongly on the subject.

SOPHIE. I'm sorry for your friend. I am *profoundly* sorry for
everybody who suffered and died on that terrible day. But

justifying isn't what I was doing. Trying to understand, perhaps. I think there's a marked difference.

ANNIE. So there are things I'm just not interested in listening to.

SOPHIE. So that history doesn't keep repeating itself –

ANNIE. Because I have that personal connection.

SOPHIE. – over and over again.

Awkward pause.

LAWRENCE. Wonderful. Thank you for taking a giant leak on the most important day of my life.

TOM. She wasn't really your friend, honey.

ANNIE. What?

TOM. I mean, you said you knew her coz you'd met her at Sarah Phillips's party in the Hamptons.

ANNIE. I saw her two weeks before she died.

TOM. I know you did, but you said you didn't like her very much. I mean, I think that's what you said.

ANNIE. I don't remember saying that.

TOM. But you only met her on that one occasion. For about fifteen minutes.

ANNIE. It was longer.

SEBASTIAN. It's funny how there are these buildings, edifices, constructions.

SOPHIE. What constructions?

SEBASTIAN. That come to signify empires, ideologies, whole economic and political systems.

TOM. What about them?

SEBASTIAN. And maybe, Tom, you are right about twentieth-century history, when the Berlin Wall came down that marked the end of Marxism, at least in the way that it had been exercised until then.

TOM. Not all that successfully, yes.

SEBASTIAN. But maybe the Twin Towers were the Berlin Wall of a certain type of capitalism, only it might take a little bit longer to acknowledge this.

SOPHIE. Because there's a lot more to be lost.

TOM. Well, in that case, I just hope your students are doing their homework.

LAWRENCE. Okay, you know what, stop, you are at a gay do. Show a little respect, for God's sake. I am about to make a very important speech.

TOM. Apologies.

LAWRENCE. So, the second bit. This is what I can remember.

SOPHIE. Go for it.

LAWRENCE (*reading from the paper*). 'Since then we have become completely domesticated and are excelling at impersonating our straightest friends. Next thing you know we'll be shopping at Morrisons and watching *Top Gear*. Which brings us to today. Here we are, bouquets, cakes, drunken relatives and all. We have arrived. It's official.

Opposites attract, they say. Looking at us you may think we're peas in a pod but believe me, appearances are deceptive. I'm Prada to Luke's Primark. I like oysters, he likes Nando's; I admire Buñuel, he's more *Naked Gun Three*. Somewhere between those two extremes there's that thing called common territory. Meet me there, Luke.'

ANNIE. That's beautiful.

SOPHIE. I told you that you hadn't forgotten it.

LAWRENCE. It's an abbreviated version but it will have to do. Follow me. I need an audience to laugh at all appropriate moments. And then weep copiously towards the end.

SEBASTIAN. We will do our best.

TOM. We shall, we shall.

LAWRENCE. And generally support with loving vibes.

ANNIE (*aside to* TOM). I can't believe you did that.

SEBASTIAN. We need to fill our glasses so we have some for the toast.

LAWRENCE. Annie, come with me, darling, let's talk interiors.

They start to make their way towards the door. They all head out, but SOPHIE *and* TOM *are towards the back.*

TOM. Sophie.

SOPHIE. Tom.

TOM. Just wait. Please. Just one second.

SOPHIE. What?

TOM. I just need to tell you something. One thing. In private.

SOPHIE. I'm listening.

Pause. They are alone.

TOM. Hello, Sophie.

SOPHIE. Hello, Tom.

TOM. You look well.

SOPHIE. I do?

TOM. Beautiful, I mean beautiful.

SOPHIE. Thank you, Tom.

Pause.

Is that what you needed to tell me?

SEBASTIAN *returns, sticks his head round the door.*

SEBASTIAN. Sophie, come, we'll miss the speeches.

SOPHIE. Yes.

SEBASTIAN. Come on, hurry.

TOM. Yes, we were coming. I just wanted –

SOPHIE. Just one minute, Sebastian. I'll be there in a minute.

SEBASTIAN *looks uncertain.*

SEBASTIAN. I'll keep your seat.

SOPHIE. Thank you.

Reluctantly, he goes.

TOM. I don't think he likes me.

SOPHIE. He has his reasons.

TOM. Can you tell him I'm a Democrat?

SOPHIE. It wouldn't make a difference.

TOM. Wouldn't it?

SOPHIE. His father was one of Allende's ministers. Two years after the coup, he committed suicide. He has issues.

TOM. I wasn't born in 1973.

SOPHIE. I'll pass it on.

Pause.

TOM. We were young.

SOPHIE. Yes.

TOM. And foolish.

SOPHIE. Yes, you were.

Pause.

TOM. How long have you and Sebastian…?

SOPHIE. A year and a half.

TOM. Not that long.

SOPHIE. He loves me. We love each other.

Pause.

We should get back.

TOM. I only flew over because I was hoping you might be here.

SOPHIE. I don't –

TOM. I was curious, is what I'm saying.

SOPHIE. Oh.

TOM. Curious to see you again. I can't lie.

Pause.

A year and a half isn't a long time, whatever you say.

SOPHIE. What are you talking about?

TOM. And then just now you said, 'He loves me,' and then a second later you added, 'We love each other.' Like an afterthought.

SOPHIE. Are you drunk?

TOM. I think so, yes. Are you?

She doesn't answer.

And if you want me to be honest –

SOPHIE. Why start now?

TOM. I don't think it's the same.

SOPHIE. What do you know about my life? About Sebastian? About me?

TOM. It's what I feel.

SOPHIE. And so to hell with everything else.

TOM. Yes.

SOPHIE. With everyone else.

TOM. It's how I feel.

Pause.

And maybe it's because we're here –

SOPHIE. What is?

TOM. But you must admit from the minute when we were both in this room and maybe if I hadn't drunk, I wasn't drunk I wouldn't be saying these things and maybe it is disloyal to Annie and low and I don't know, unfair or something –

SOPHIE. It is.

TOM. Reptilian, but from the moment we were in this room and we were making jokes and talking about what we all do and how we all were and blah blah blah but from the moment we were in the same room it was as if no time had passed and then maybe we could be back in New York and we wouldn't make the same choices –

SOPHIE. Which one of us?

TOM. But from the minute we were in the same room it was as if it was just us again, and these people we're with –

SOPHIE. Don't talk about them like that.

TOM. – were accidental in some way, or incidental, or not the real thing, and I wish them well, I wish them well, I wish them well but every so often you have to say 'this is how I feel right now' and that is all that really matters.

Pause.

What was Iraq like?

SOPHIE. Why do you care about Iraq, Tom?

TOM. Because you were there.

Pause. She thinks about it.

SOPHIE. I don't think Annie meant any harm by saying that that poor woman was her friend.

TOM. No.

SOPHIE. I think what she meant was 'We were alike. We shopped at the same places, and dressed in similar ways and knew the same people.' I think that's what she meant.

TOM. I think you're right.

SOPHIE. Well, in Iraq they don't shop at the same places or dress in similar ways or maybe know the same people. That's all.

Pause.

That's what Iraq was like.

TOM. Yes.

SOPHIE. And a little dustier.

TOM. Sophie.

SOPHIE. I did think about you when I was there. One night. I don't know why. I'd been with this girl for about a week. Her name was Janan. She… her parents had. Her father was. So she was orphaned. Living with this aunt on the outskirts of Baghdad. I became quite close to her. Inevitably. The things she'd lived through. So this one night after I'd been with Janan I returned to my hotel and I lay in my dark bedroom and I stared at the fan on the ceiling whirring around my head and I thought of you. I felt like I was going to be stuck in that room for the whole of eternity and I thought: come and find me and take me away, Tom. Buy me nice things, take me everywhere. I thought, fuck her. Fuck Janan. Fuck the children, who cares if they're disabled or damaged or dying or dead? Fucking fuck 'em. I didn't give a flying fuck. I wanted to be with you. That's all. It's all I wanted. With you and wearing something nice.

Pause.

I envy Annie.

Pause.

TOM. I don't think a single day goes by when I don't think of you in some way or another.

She throws her glass of wine in his face.

Okay.

SEBASTIAN *returns.*

SEBASTIAN. You are still here.

SOPHIE. Yes. We got stuck.

SEBASTIAN. You all right?

SOPHIE. We're fine, we're fine.

TOM. I'll see you later.

SOPHIE. Yes, yes, later.

TOM *leaves. There is a pause.*

The answer is yes.

SEBASTIAN. Yes, what?

SOPHIE. To what you were about to ask me. To what your mother wants. To bourgeois convention.

SEBASTIAN. Yes?

SOPHIE. Yes, yes, yes.

SEBASTIAN. Fuck.

SOPHIE. The answer is yes.

He walks up to her; they kiss.

SEBASTIAN. I love you.

SOPHIE. I just need another minute.

SEBASTIAN. Cool. And then come and dance with me. Barefoot.

He starts to walk out of the room, stops. Punches the air triumphantly.

I'm going to go call Chile!

He leaves the room. She stands silently.

EDWARD *walks into the room.* SOPHIE *cannot see him. He is looking much older than when we last saw him and more dishevelled. He is holding a tattered old copy of the Bible and reciting from it in a loud, meandering voice. Slowly, brushing past him on the way,* SOPHIE *leaves the room.*

EDWARD (*reading*). 'One Sabbath he was going through the grain fields; and as they made their way his disciples began to pluck heads of grain. The Pharisees said to him: "Look, why are they doing what is not lawful on the Sabbath?" And he said to them: "Have you never read what David did when he and his companions were hungry and in need of food? He entered the house of God, when Abiathar was high priest, and ate the bread of the Presence, which is not lawful for any but the priest to eat, and he gave some to his companions." Then he said to them, "The Sabbath was made for humankind and not humankind for the Sabbath." '

Scene Two

2001

EDWARD *comes to stand in the middle of the space. Around him, the scene changes. The room fades and we are back in Patmos, an early spring evening.*

He wanders off, book in hand. TATYANA *enters, followed by* SOPHIE *and* TOM, *who is carrying a small case.*

TATYANA. He no listen to me, Miss Sophie. Never listen. I say 'Eat, Mister Edward, eat, in life you must eat' –

TOM. It helps.

TATYANA. But he no eat. Then he is always shouting. He is scaring me.

SOPHIE. Of course.

TATYANA. In only two years since he leave the Church everything stops working. He becomes crazy and all so quickly.

SOPHIE. He's had two strokes, Tatyana, that's why.

TATYANA. And then you know, there is the new problem.

SOPHIE. New problem?

TATYANA. How you say in English? У него недержание. [*Pronounced: 'U nevo ne-der-zha-ni-e.' Meaning: 'He is incontinent.'*] The poo.

SOPHIE. The what?

TATYANA. The poo. He does the poo-poo. под себя. [*Pronounced: 'Pad-sebia.' Meaning: 'On himself.'*] On himself.

SOPHIE. Okay.

TOM. Shit.

TATYANA. Yes, Tom, the shit, I know.

TOM. That's a whole new territory.

TATYANA. In his trousers, Miss Sophie.

SOPHIE. But surely he's wearing a pad.

TATYANA. Yes, Miss Sophie, he is wearing the pad but then he no let me change. He shout at me. 'Go away, Tatyana, leave me, I no need you.' Но оно ведь пахнет. [*Pronounced: 'No ono ved' pakh-net.' Meaning: 'But it smells.'*] But it smells, Miss Sophie, because he not let me change them.

SOPHIE. The minute you called we got on the flight. And I've made a few phone calls.

TATYANA. Yes, Miss Sophie.

SOPHIE. There's a home. In Athens. It's clean, pleasant –

TOM. It's perfect.

TATYANA. A home?

SOPHIE. For my father, I mean.

TOM. We're going to take him there. On Tuesday.

SOPHIE. But you need to know that you can stay here and we'll keep your salary going –

TOM. We'll definitely do that.

SOPHIE. So that you can look after the place and then when, if, you find somewhere else –

TOM. Only if you want to.

SOPHIE. Well, then you can go. But not unless you want to.

TATYANA (*fighting the tears*). Thank you, Miss Sophie, Mister Tom. You are golden, like your father.

SOPHIE. Now we need to sort out quite a few practical things.

EDWARD *drifts on, looking lost.*

EDWARD. Sophia.

SOPHIE. Hello, Dad.

EDWARD. Sophia.

TOM. Hello, Edward.

SOPHIE. You remember Tom, Dad?

EDWARD *looks at him blankly.*

TOM. Well, I remember you.

TATYANA. You see how crazy he looks?

SOPHIE. Why don't you go and have a rest, Tatyana.

TATYANA. I go make courgette pie. You call if you need me.

TOM. I love your pies.

SOPHIE. Thank you, Tatyana.

TATYANA *moves to go. Then she turns to* EDWARD.

TATYANA. Now you do what Miss Sophie says. And you no shout at her like you shout at me, Edward. Все время кричишь. [*Pronounced: 'Vse vremia kri-chish.' Meaning: 'Always shouting.'*]

EDWARD. I AM LIFE!

TATYANA *leaves.*

'Edward this, Edward that, Edward, Edward, Edward, Edward, you smell, Edward, Edward, Edward,' and I say to her, I say to her –

SOPHIE. What do you say to her, Dad?

EDWARD. I say to her, 'I am not Edward, so don't call me that, stop calling me it' –

SOPHIE. So who are you, Dad?

EDWARD. I AM LIFE!

TOM. Okay, Edward, no one's arguing with you.

SOPHIE. So, Life, do I get a kiss?

SOPHIE *walks up to him and puts her arms around him, kisses him.*

We came all the way from New York, Dad.

TOM. Just to see you. And so far, you haven't disappointed.

EDWARD. How's your book?

TOM. My book? You remember my book?

SOPHIE. He remembers your book.

TOM. Edward, I'm impressed.

EDWARD. How is it?

TOM. Oh, you know, simmering away.

TOM *imitates* SOPHIE, *gives him a slightly awkward hug.*

SOPHIE. I've missed you, Dad.

TOM (*aside to* SOPHIE). Okay, we need to talk.

SOPHIE. I know.

TOM. It's bad.

SOPHIE. I know it is.

TOM. And we are *outdoors*.

EDWARD. Sophia.

SOPHIE. What is it, Dad?

EDWARD. My daughter Sophia.

SOPHIE *surveys the situation.*

SOPHIE. Okay, Dad. You're not going to like this but we need to give you a wash.

TOM. *We?*

EDWARD. I AM LIFE!

SOPHIE. I know, Dad, I know you're Life but you need to do what I tell you for a few minutes. Come with me, Dad.

She tries to lead him indoors but he resists.

EDWARD. Don't you bloody start.

SOPHIE. Please, Dad.

EDWARD. I'm not going anywhere.

SOPHIE. Just for a while.

EDWARD. Unhand me.

SOPHIE. Please, Dad.

EDWARD. I want the sun.

TOM. He wants the sun.

SOPHIE. Okay, so we'll do it here.

TOM. *Here?*

SOPHIE. I'm not fighting a battle to get him inside and maybe it's better outdoors. Ask Tatyana to give you whatever you need.

TOM (*pulls* SOPHIE *to one side*). Sophie, I need to talk to you a minute.

SOPHIE. Go on.

TOM. The fact is, I don't know how to say this but –

SOPHIE. But what?

TOM. I'm not a fan of shit.

SOPHIE. You'll find that it's a very select minority of people who actually are.

TOM. You know I have a terrible gag-reflex thing.

SOPHIE. Just get the stuff.

TOM. That's all you need. Shit *and* vomit.

SOPHIE. Okay, Tom, *listen*. I am not expecting you to be an active member of this adventure. I know you well enough. I'm just asking you to get me a bucket of water, the disinfectant soap, the wash rag and whatever else Tatyana gives you. That is all, I promise.

TOM. I'm sorry.

SOPHIE. Just go.

TOM. Faster than an arrow from a Tartar's bow.

He goes.

EDWARD. I need to talk to you.

SOPHIE. What about, Dad?

EDWARD. Cornelius.

SOPHIE. Cornelius?

EDWARD. Acts of the Apostles.

SOPHIE. Oh, *that* Cornelius.

EDWARD. Everything evolves.

SOPHIE. I know, Dad, I agree, everything does evolve.

EDWARD. *Changes*, it has to, in order to survive.

SOPHIE. I know, Dad.

EDWARD. I am Life.

SOPHIE. I know you are.

EDWARD. Moving *towards*.

Pause.

SOPHIE. Look. The gulls. Can you see them? Diving into the sea.

EDWARD. For fish.

SOPHIE. Yes, fish.

Pause.

Okay, I need you to listen to me, it's important. Tom has gone to get some water and a clean pad. We need to change you, Dad, because… we need to change you. Please, just let me do that and then we can sit down, talk, whatever, walk in the garden, whatever you like. But please don't make a fuss. I need to change the pad and I'm asking you to cooperate.

EDWARD. It's come to that.

SOPHIE. Yes, I'm afraid it has. It's come to that.

TOM *comes back, bucket, pad and soap in hand.*

TOM. Operation De-shitification of Life is ready, Thunderbirds are go.

SOPHIE. Put them down there.

TOM. I can stand here and make sure people don't walk by. Or if they do, I can throw things at them.

SOPHIE. Tom.

She leads EDWARD *towards a bench.*

Sit here, Dad.

EDWARD. Only connect.

TOM. We're definitely about to connect, Edward.

EDWARD *sits.*

SOPHIE. Actually, Dad, wait, I need you to stand.

EDWARD. You said sit.

TOM. She's changed her mind, it happens.

SOPHIE. Sorry, Dad, I need to take your trousers off and I can't do it if you're sitting down.

EDWARD *stands and she starts unbuttoning his trousers.*

TOM. This is the bit where I go check if people are walking by.

SOPHIE. Open the soap thing.

TOM. Because that reflex is definitely starting to act up.

SOPHIE. Tom, I need you to do that.

TOM. Okay, sweetie.

SOPHIE. And moisten the rag, I mean wet it.

TOM. Wet the rag, Thomas, wet the rag. Focus on the rag.

He unscrews the bottled soap and dunks the rag in the bowl of water, while she starts to help EDWARD *step out of his trousers.*

SOPHIE. Okay, Dad, easy.

EDWARD. 'And there came a voice to him saying, "Rise, Peter, kill and eat," but Peter said, "Not so, Lord, for I have never eaten anything that is common or unclean," and the voice spake again the second time and said, "What God hath cleansed, that call not thou common."'

TOM. Okay, so a little scripture to distract us.

SOPHIE. Now sit down, Dad.

He sits.

EDWARD. Everything evolves.

TOM. I'm evolving as we speak.

EDWARD. The body, the mind, the soul, the grass, the earth.

TOM. I am definitely evolving here.

EDWARD. Nothing is stationary, nothing still.

SOPHIE. Give me the rag.

TOM *hands her the rag.*

Stand up, Dad.

EDWARD. You said sit.

SOPHIE. I need you to stand.

EDWARD *stands.*

TOM. He's the human yo-yo.

SOPHIE. Okay, you may want to look away, crunch time.

TOM. Oh, Jesus, yes, thank you, and deep breath in.

EDWARD. Love suffereth long and is kind.

SOPHIE. And pad is coming off.

TOM. Oh. Jesus. Fuck. No.

We see her taking off the pad.

SOPHIE. Where's the empty bowl?

TOM. What empty bowl?

SOPHIE. I need somewhere for the used pad.

TOM. You didn't say anything about an empty bowl.

SOPHIE. Shit.

TOM. Lots of it.

EDWARD. I AM LIFE.

TOM. You are definitely Life, Edward, you are definitely Life.

SOPHIE. I can't just put them on the floor.

TOM. In all its glory.

SOPHIE. I need a bowl, a bucket, something.

EDWARD. Love vaunteth not itself, is not puffed up.

TOM. Neither am I.

SOPHIE. Tom.

TOM. We're outdoors, put it on the floor and we'll sort it out later.

She places the used pad on the floor.

EDWARD. Beareth all things, believeth all things, hopeth all things, endureth all things.

TOM. It certainly does.

SOPHIE. Okay, step two.

The sound of a mobile phone ringing.

TOM. Jesus, the timing.

He takes his phone out, looks at it.

It's Roger, I need to answer it.

SOPHIE. Roger?

TOM. Hartmann, from the office. The Maybelline job. It's the deadline.

SOPHIE. Maybelline?

TOM. I need to answer it.

SOPHIE. Tom, I am holding my father's… in my hand, I can't hold him, I need you to be with me right now.

TOM. I told you before, Sophie, that if Roger called I needed to answer it, I promised him I was only going to Greece on the condition that I answered his calls. He's fine, you're fine, Edward, he's fine.

SOPHIE. Tom, I need you to hold him…

TOM. Thirty seconds.

He answers the phone, moves away from SOPHIE *and* EDWARD. SOPHIE *puts the dirty pad on the floor and starts cleaning* EDWARD *with the rag.*

(*Into the phone.*) Roger, yes, hi. We are, we are. Oh, you know, stuff. Doing stuff.

No, that's cool, I was just… it's fine, I can talk.

SOPHIE. No, you can't.

TOM. No, I left the proposals with Michelle. Did you see them? Oh, you did? Great. I'm happy you like them.

EDWARD. Though I have the gift of prophecy, and understand all mysteries –

TOM. What's that? Yes, I think so too. Dynamic, definitely.

EDWARD. And all knowledge –

TOM. And provocative too in a kind of young kind of way, I know… Hold on, Roger, can you just wait one second, thank you.

EDWARD. And though I have all faith so that I can remove all mountains –

TOM. Can you just, ask him to be quiet? Just like for thirty seconds, *please*, Edward –

SOPHIE. Go inside, why don't you go inside.

EDWARD. For we know in part and we prophecy in part –

TOM. You know that this is like the only spot on the whole goddamned island where I get a signal –

SOPHIE. Tough.

TOM (*into phone*). No, I'm still here, Roger, there's a problem with… em, with the signal, the signal is shit, I mean, the signal is bad, just hold on.

EDWARD. But when that which is perfect is come, then that which is in part shall be done away.

TOM. Can you not take him, I mean, finish inside? *I beg you*.

SOPHIE. TOM, I AM WIPING MY FATHER'S ARSE CLEAN, I CANNOT MOVE INSIDE.

TOM (*into phone*). No, that's fine, just interference, I can hear you fine.

EDWARD. When I was a child I spake as a child –

TOM (*into phone*). Sexier? How d'you mean sexier? Okay, cool.

SOPHIE. Why can't you ask him to call you back in five minutes?

EDWARD. I understood as a child, I thought as a child –

TOM (*into phone*). No, definitely, I know where you're coming from, young, innocent but also kind of you know, womanly, or at least more sophisticated.

EDWARD. But when I became a man I put away childish things.

TOM (*into phone*). No, not in a whorey way, good God no, but I mean, sexy yes, sort of beautiful and shall we say… nymphic, I don't know, is that a word, nymphic –

SOPHIE. Nymphic.

TOM (*into phone*). No, not lymphic as in lymph nodes, I said nymphic as in nymphs, you know, mythological spirits of nature –

EDWARD. For now we see things through a glass darkly, but then face to face.

TOM (*into phone*). As in maiden-like creatures.

SOPHIE. Maiden-like creatures.

TOM (*into phone*). I completely agree with you, cool.

EDWARD. Now I know in part, but then shall I know even as also I am known.

TOM (*into phone*). We're back in Athens Tuesday, I'll be landing in New York Wednesday afternoon. Cool. I'll call you the minute I land, thanks, Roger.

SOPHIE. Thanks, Roger.

TOM turns off his phone.

EDWARD. And now abideth faith, hope, love, these three.

SOPHIE. But the greatest of these is love. Thanks, Dad.

She rinses out the rag.

(*To* TOM.) Could you pass me the clean pad, please?

TOM. Sure.

TOM goes back to where they are and hands her the clean pad. None of them speak as she starts putting the clean pad on, then thoroughly washes her hands and then her father's too.

I had to take that.

SOPHIE. Can you take all the stuff back in, please.

TOM. Sure I can.

He picks up the bowl, the soap, everything excluding the used pad.

SOPHIE. Including the used pad.

He hesitates, then picks it up with great difficulty. It looks as if he's gagging.

We're finished, Dad. That was easy enough.

TOM is walking off with everything in hand.

TOM. Oh, Jesus, I'm going to be sick.

SOPHIE. And bring a pair of underwear and some trousers from his room. The big cupboard in the corner. Underwear second drawer down.

TOM runs off, his hands full, gagging as he goes.

Let's sit down. Sunset time.

EDWARD. Sunset time.

They sit on the bench. He is just in his shirt and pad.

SOPHIE. That's better, isn't it.

EDWARD. Better, better.

They look out.

They take it all literally.

SOPHIE. Yes.

EDWARD. Fools, fools, fools. Myths, poetry, myths, poetry, myths, poetry.

SOPHIE. I know.

EDWARD. Understanding it.

SOPHIE. Understanding what, Dad?

EDWARD. The soul of the world. Not the way they try. Fools. Sisters.

SOPHIE. Sisters?

EDWARD. Religion and art. Sisters.

SOPHIE. Okay, Dad.

EDWARD. And on the other side, the others.

SOPHIE. What others?

EDWARD. The militant atheist saying, 'Don't think like that, don't dream like that, don't wish like that, don't breathe like that.'

SOPHIE. Yes.

EDWARD. Like the right hand asking the left hand not to move.

SOPHIE. Oh.

EDWARD. The right hand saying to the left hand, 'Stop moving, stop moving, stop moving.'

SOPHIE. I see.

EDWARD. As if it can. As if the left hand can ever stop moving.

SOPHIE. No, I know, it can't.

EDWARD. As if it has a choice.

SOPHIE. It doesn't.

EDWARD. Fools.

SOPHIE. Yes.

Pause.

EDWARD. I'm sorry you had to. You know. I'm sorry. Stink of shit.

SOPHIE. No you don't.

Pause. Then EDWARD *starts to weep. She lets him.* TOM *comes back. He's carrying some underwear and a pair of trousers.*

TOM. Here you go.

He hands her the underwear and trousers.

SOPHIE. Come on, Dad. Let's get you dressed.

EDWARD. No.

TOM. Stand up, Edward, so we can get these boxers on.

TOM *helps him up slowly.* EDWARD *leans against* TOM *while* SOPHIE *manoeuvres the underwear around his ankles and up to his waist.*

I'm sorry but I really needed to take that call.

SOPHIE. You said.

TOM. It was important.

SOPHIE. It sounded it.

TOM. So I needed to take it.

SOPHIE. Let's just change the subject, shall we?

Pause. They keep on dressing him. EDWARD *suddenly abandons emotion and becomes very matter-of-fact.*

EDWARD. I need to speak to you.

SOPHIE. I'm listening.

EDWARD. My book.

SOPHIE. Which book, Dad?

EDWARD. The one I'm writing. Someone needs to finish it.

SOPHIE. You're writing a book?

EDWARD. The publishers are waiting.

SOPHIE. Are they?

EDWARD. It's revolutionary.

TOM. We expect nothing less.

EDWARD. Important.

SOPHIE. I'm sure, Dad.

TOM. And now for the trousers, Edward.

> TOM *hands the trousers to* SOPHIE, *who starts putting them on for* EDWARD. *Again* TOM *is holding him, making sure he doesn't lose his balance.*

EDWARD. I've left notes. Pieces of paper.

SOPHIE. Okay.

TOM. Pieces of paper?

EDWARD. Everywhere. Under the bed. In the hole.

SOPHIE. What hole?

EDWARD. You must find them.

TOM. A theological treasure hunt. What fun.

EDWARD. Here it is. Read it.

> *He takes a crumpled piece of paper out of his shirt pocket, and hands it to* TOM, *who reads it.*

TOM. '*The patriarchal gods will die*.' Not until they've put up a damn good fight, I'm sure.

EDWARD. Will you do that, Sophia?

SOPHIE. Do what, Dad?

EDWARD. Find the pieces. Finish the book.

SOPHIE. I can't, Dad.

EDWARD. Why? Why? Why?

SOPHIE. I can't finish your book, Dad.

EDWARD. Fuck it.

SOPHIE. After all, it's your book, Dad, it isn't mine.

EDWARD. What about the American?

TOM. You don't have to talk about me in the third person, Edward, I'm here.

SOPHIE. No, he works in advertising.

TOM. Did you have to tell him that?

SOPHIE. I'm sorry, Dad, I wish we could, but we can't. We can't write your book.

Pause.

EDWARD. Then do something else for me.

SOPHIE. What?

EDWARD. Remember me.

She's taken aback.

SOPHIE. Of course. Of course I'll remember you.

Pause.

EDWARD. He works in *advertising*?

TATYANA comes back.

TATYANA. You have changed him. The pad.

SOPHIE. Yes.

TATYANA. Edward, why you not let me change you? Why you let Sophie do it? When I say to you, 'Let me change you, Edward' –

EDWARD. Shut up.

TATYANA. Why you say, 'No, no, no, get away, get away from me, Tatyana'? Why you do this, Edward?

EDWARD. See what I mean?

SOPHIE. Maybe you shouldn't, I don't know, talk to him like that.

TATYANA. Why do you do this, Edward?

SOPHIE. Like a child, I mean. Please don't. Talk to him like that.

TOM. She's just trying to help, Sophie.

SOPHIE. I'm sorry. I didn't want. It's just that he's not a child, Tatyana.

TATYANA. He's like a child.

SOPHIE. But he isn't. He isn't a child. So maybe you shouldn't talk to him as if he were one.

Pause.

I'm sorry. I just needed to say that.

TATYANA. It is difficult because I am here all the time. Попробуй(те) поживи(те) с ним. [*Pronounced: 'Pah-proh-boo-ee-tyeh pah-zhee-vee-tyeh sneem.' Meaning: 'You try living with him.'*] Edward and Tatyana. Just the two of us. So maybe I forget. This is why.

SOPHIE. Yes.

Pause. EDWARD is staring at TOM.

TOM (*to SOPHIE*). You know when we started dating I never imagined, you know… but this is good, this is definitely good. Getting to know you and your family. It's just I never imagined it like this.

SOPHIE. Didn't you?

EDWARD *keeps staring.*

TOM. Some say staring at people like the way you're staring at me now, Edward, is bordering on rude.

EDWARD *keeps staring.*

But maybe it's just a culture thing. In America, that is definitely rude. But here, in the isles of Greece, perhaps it's considered a mark of respect, who knows.

EDWARD. Thomas.

TOM. I'll be damned.

EDWARD. Doubting Thomas.

TOM. Are you getting personal?

EDWARD. Thomas, Thomas. Thomas.

TOM. Edward, Edward, Edward.

EDWARD. Matter will yield but only when we're ready.

TOM. If you say so.

EDWARD. The dormant powers of the human mind.

TOM. 'Dormant', interesting choice of word.

EDWARD. Help me.

TOM. Your wish is my command.

EDWARD. The book. I need to finish the book.

TOM. And how can I help you do that?

EDWARD. The papers, find the papers.

TATYANA. Everywhere in the house little pieces of paper.

SOPHIE. Which paper do you mean, Dad?

EDWARD. They're here, somewhere here.

SOPHIE. Dad?

TATYANA. He writes little pieces –

SOPHIE. Like the one he showed us.

TATYANA. And everywhere in the house. Маленькие бумажки сводят меня с ума. [*Pronounced: 'Ma-len'-ki-e bumazhki svo-diat menia syma.' Meaning: 'Little pieces of paper, driving me crazy.'*]

EDWARD *stands up and starts to scurry about looking for his piece of paper – under the bench, under pots, on the floor – he becomes increasingly distressed.*

EDWARD. Help me find it, Thomas, help me find it.

TOM. I need to know what it is we're looking for, Edward.

EDWARD. Paper, paper.

TOM. I need you to be more specific.

SOPHIE. A little piece of paper like the one he gave you earlier.

TOM. And I mean we're actually looking now? Or are we just pretending to look?

EDWARD. Find the paper, find the paper.

TOM. I'm looking, Edward, I'm looking.

TOM *starts looking, imitating* EDWARD, *who is becoming more and more distressed.*

EDWARD. Quickly, quickly, quickly, paper, paper, paper.

SOPHIE *goes up to him, tries to calm him.*

SOPHIE. It's okay, Dad, we'll find it, we'll find the paper, try not to –

EDWARD. I need the paper, I need the paper, I need the paper –

TOM. I'm working on it, Edward.

EDWARD. I need the paper.

SOPHIE. Please, Dad.

EDWARD. THE PAPER, THE PAPER, THE PAPER, I NEED THE PAPER!

He collapses into SOPHIE*'s arms and begins to sob.*

SOPHIE. It's okay, it's okay, it's okay. I have you now, I have you now, I have you now. Shhh.

TATYANA. Every day like this. Каждый день. [*Pronounced: 'Kazh-dui den.' Meaning: 'Every day.'*]

Pause. And then TOM, *who had been searching through a flowerpot, raises his hand. He's holding a tiny piece of paper.*

TOM. Well, I'll be damned.

SOPHIE. Look, Dad, Tom's found the piece of paper.

TOM. I found it! I found it! I found it!

SOPHIE. Thank you, Tom.

TATYANA. Everywhere in the house pieces of paper. Повсюду. [*Pronounced: 'Povsudu.' Meaning: 'Everywhere.'*]

EDWARD. Read it.

TOM. Yes, sir.

He opens it. It is obviously blank. He turns it over. Blank, both sides. He looks in panic at SOPHIE.

(*Mouthing.*) It's blank. Nothing on it.

SOPHIE (*prompting him to make something up*). What does it say, Tom?

TOM (*stalling*). You mean the paper? What does the paper say?

SOPHIE. Yes, what does it say?

EDWARD. What does it say? What does it say? WHAT DOES IT SAY?

EDWARD *is waiting for the response.* TOM *takes a deep breath, stalls, improvises, but not with great conviction.*

TOM. 'Seek, and ye shall find'?

Blackout.

End of Act Two.

ACT THREE

Scene One

2010

A hotel room. Slick, impersonal. A bed, a chair, a plasma television screen and not much else.

It is a winter evening in London and maybe there is a snow falling outside.

SOPHIE *and* TOM *are under the sheets, making love. A lot of noise comes from the pair but most of it suggests discomfort, not pleasure. Then, finally:*

SOPHIE. Ow.

TOM. What's wrong?

SOPHIE. Something's hurting me.

TOM. What is?

SOPHIE. I don't know, something's in my back.

Suddenly the television switches on. It's BBC World News. *A news report: the date is mentioned and so is the year and then something about the financial situation caused by the banking crisis and about the cuts being made in the UK by the Coalition Government.*

It's the remote.

TOM. You turned the TV on.

SOPHIE. Not on purpose.

TOM. Am I boring you?

SOPHIE. Just turn it off.

TOM. Where is it? Where is the remote?

SOPHIE. It's near my bra. I can feel it.

TOM. Okay, wait.

There is some fumbling about. Then, suddenly the television switches off.

Oh, shit.

SOPHIE. What?

TOM. My watch is caught on your bra thing.

SOPHIE. What bra thing?

TOM. Your bra clasp.

SOPHIE. Well, undo... *ow*... undo it, Tom.

TOM. Can you just lie still until I do this?

SOPHIE. I am lying still.

TOM. Just wait.

There is fumbling about.

I can't get it off.

SOPHIE. You can't get what off?

TOM. The watch. I don't know what happened. I think what happened is it opened up. And then snapped shut again but kind of did it when the bra clasp was in the way.

SOPHIE. Well, take it off.

TOM. That's what I'm doing, Sophie.

More fumbling.

You have to take your bra off, Sophie.

SOPHIE. How can I take my bra off when your whole arm is in it?

TOM. We have to get out of bed.

They crawl out of bed. TOM*'s hand is attached to her bra clasp. It's like a game of Twister.*

Foreplay improves with age.

They struggle around a little but to no avail.

Maybe we should call someone. Like reception, or something.

SOPHIE. That's a great idea, Tom.

TOM. 'Hello, sir, my lady friend and I seem to have got ourselves into a little bind here. Would you mind unclasping us?'

SOPHIE. I need to see what I'm doing, then maybe I can undo the bra.

TOM. Okay, so let's do that.

SOPHIE. I need a mirror.

TOM. The bathroom.

SOPHIE. Okay.

They hobble off into the bathroom. The next lines are spoken offstage.

Can you just stop moving for a second?

TOM. I'm not moving.

SOPHIE. Just keep your hand still.

TOM. I am. At least I'm trying to.

SOPHIE. That's better. Now I can see what I'm doing.

A little more struggling.

There.

TOM. Jesus.

SOPHIE. I need.

TOM. What? You need what?

SOPHIE. Can you just close the door, please.

The door closes. Then it opens again.

No, I mean, with you on the outside.

TOM *steps back into the room.*

TOM. You don't want to resume our… that thing we were doing? Before the watch incident?

SOPHIE. Please, Tom. Just a minute.

She closes the door. He stands outside it.

TOM. Are you okay? Because I have a distinct feeling I've lost you.

No reply.

It's not adultery. I'm divorced and you. Well, you said Sebastian and you were. Temporarily separated. After the incident with the French student. (*Sotto voce to himself.*) Private tutorials in Marxist theory.

Still no response.

It would be good if you could give me some sort of clue. A pointer. Like, I don't know: 'This wasn't a good idea because of your breath, Tom. Or that thing you said.' Or: 'You're a constant disappointment.' I don't know. Whatever. Just something.

She comes out of the bathroom wearing a bathrobe. She aims straight for the chair her clothes are on and begins to get dressed. Her actions have a purpose to them, as if all of a sudden she is in a hurry.

SOPHIE. Your breath is fine and no, it wasn't anything you said.

TOM. What then?

She continues to get dressed.

SOPHIE. I have something that belongs to you.

TOM. How exciting.

SOPHIE. I was clearing out some old boxes. In my study.

TOM. Okay.

SOPHIE. And I found this.

She opens her bag, takes out a manuscript, hands it to him. She returns to getting dressed.

TOM. Fuck.

SOPHIE. I thought you'd appreciate it.

TOM. '*The Missing Man*'.

SOPHIE. With your own notes in the margins.

She keeps dressing. He flicks through the manuscript.

TOM. Tolstoyan in its ambition if a little clunky.

SOPHIE. It was your first completed novel, Tom. You were twenty-four. It's not going to be *War and Peace*.

TOM. Did you call me nine years after we broke up to discuss the promise in my writing?

SOPHIE. It's a first draft. Maybe one day you'll work on the second one.

TOM. Unlikely.

SOPHIE. I know it is. After all, you're not very good at sticking to things.

TOM. I was good a minute ago.

SOPHIE. Seeing things through.

TOM. When I was stuck to your bra, I mean.

SOPHIE. Yes, you were good at that. And you're consistently good in seeing the lighter side of everything.

She makes a move to go. He runs to the door and blocks it.

TOM. You can't go. Not now. Not like this.

SOPHIE. Tom, get out of the way.

TOM. You call me up, you say –

SOPHIE. I know I called you.

TOM. 'When you're next in town, Tom' –

SOPHIE. It was a mistake, I said so –

TOM. 'I need to see you, Tom.'

SOPHIE. I thought I did.

TOM. And then you say, 'Let's go to the room,' I didn't drag you here –

SOPHIE. I didn't say you did.

TOM. You suggested it.

SOPHIE. I know, I know I did.

TOM. And now you're like 'I'm leaving.'

SOPHIE. I need to.

TOM. Not before you talk to me.

SOPHIE. Please get out of my way, Tom.

TOM. Before you explain.

SOPHIE. You don't want to hear what I have to say.

TOM. Because you can't keep doing this, Sophie.

SOPHIE. You really don't want to hear it.

TOM. Walking out on me every ten fucking years.

SOPHIE. You really don't.

TOM. BECAUSE YOU CAN'T KEEP FUCKING DOING THIS!

Pause. They are both surprised by the intensity of his reaction.
SOPHIE *takes a deep breath.*

SOPHIE. All right then.

TOM. Go on.

SOPHIE. I was hoping that when I read it I'd realise that I was
young, and in love with you and unable to be objective and that
you'd been right to give it up –

TOM. What are you talking about?

SOPHIE. But that now I'd see its flaws and agree with you and say,
'Yes, he has very little to say, he had to let it go,' but then I read it
and there was –

TOM. There was what?

SOPHIE. A *reason* you were writing.

TOM. So you called me to tell me that?

SOPHIE. And I was sitting there in the middle of the night, thinking
of why things turned out the way they did, why you lost that
belief you had in yourself and when it was that happened, when it
started *eroding* –

TOM. I have a feeling you're going to tell me.

SOPHIE. – and it was when we returned to New York and you
started the job at Hartmanns –

TOM. What about it?

SOPHIE. – and it had something to do with words losing their
definitions, their intrinsic meanings –

TOM. What the fuck are you talking about?

SOPHIE. – words like *success* and *happiness* and *aspiration*, *believe in better*, and that once the words went, then everything else did too and that things lost their shape and you weren't able to distinguish what was true from what wasn't and that was the intention and you fell for it so easily.

TOM. What intention?

SOPHIE. And that everything became not about what you were but about the way you were perceived, not about what connected you to others but about what *separated* you –

TOM. Separated me?

SOPHIE. And that, before you realised it, life had become meaningless and that every choice you made was unimportant because in a life with no meaning everything is acceptable, or laughable or weightless and everything is condoned –

TOM. Fucking hell, Sophie.

SOPHIE. And that we found ourselves in this world we had created that survived and prospered on the very fact that we no longer believed in *anything*.

TOM. Jesus Christ.

SOPHIE. And then I read your book, Tom, and it was by a boy, a boy who had this thing we call a *soul*, untutored and young and still searching, but a soul, a soul, a *soul*.

TOM. Jesus fuck.

SOPHIE. Until you sold it to the highest bidder.

Pause.

TOM. You fucking come here in judgement on me with your fucking ideals, your superiority, you fucking come here –

SOPHIE. You asked me.

TOM. And tell me these things and say words have lost their definitions, words like *success* and *happiness*, you have the fucking nerve to do that, to sit in judgement on me –

SOPHIE. That's not what I'm doing –

TOM. – you come and judge *me* and speak of souls and highest bidders –

SOPHIE. Because I knew what you were –

TOM. Well, let me tell you something now, and you listen to me, for once in your fucking life listen to me –

SOPHIE. – the things you were capable of.

TOM. – because I am going to tell you something now about how things are, not about what you'd like them to be but about the way they are, the way it is –

SOPHIE. What way?

TOM. The way it is, Sophie, the way it is, the way IT FUCKING IS.

He silences her.

Fucking atoms, fucking things, animals, fucking animals in the fucking dark, eating each other, fucking eating, killing, destroying each other, it's what we fucking are, fucking appetite that's all, ruthless and indiscriminate, floating around in a fucking universe that doesn't give a flying fuck about us, and all we fucking have, the only chance at happiness, the only fucking chance we have is to find that one fucking person who makes you want to get out of bed in the morning and we had that and you… and you fucking come to me as if *I* made the world, as if *I* fucking decided it, as if *I* chose the fucking way life is.

SOPHIE. You did, Tom.

TOM. And you talk about these words as if you know what they mean, about *happiness* as if you know what it means –

SOPHIE. I never said that.

TOM. – because excuse me if I've got the wrong picture here, forgive me if I have an erroneous idea, but from what Lawrence has told me –

SOPHIE. I never said I knew.

TOM. – from what I've heard in passing, ever since you came back from Iraq you find it difficult to get out of bed in the fucking morning, have to scrape yourself off the fucking floor –

SOPHIE. Because of what I saw –

TOM. – so excuse me for not thinking you would be the right person to consult for the most precise definition of that particular word –

SOPHIE. The *things* I saw.

TOM. Excuse me for thinking that but the fact is –

SOPHIE. And knowing that way we live, the *choices* we've made –

TOM. – that what I see in front of me is a woman who's spent her whole fucking life doing the right thing, honouring her dead fucking father, living the right way, doing the right thing –

SOPHIE. – have made us complicit.

TOM. – AT THE COST OF HAVING LIVED HER LIFE AT ALL.

Pause.

SOPHIE *slowly picks up her things, moves toward the door as if she is about to leave, then stops and turns to him.*

SOPHIE. I thought you were the one who left me.

Pause.

Afterwards I waited. I hoped. Foolishly, I know. That maybe you would change your mind. Maybe, then. The two of us. Together. Something like happiness.

She walks up to him and kisses him gently. Then she goes. He does not move for a few seconds.

Then, slowly, he walks to the chair and begins to dress. As he does, the snow ceases to fall and the scene changes around him.

Scene Two

2011

TOM *is back on the terrace in Patmos but it has changed: it has been invaded by books. They are all over the place, they have left the edges and corners of the space and have taken it over completely. In piles, in boxes, on chairs, on the floors: books everywhere.*

TATYANA *is standing in the middle of the space, dusting some of them.* TOM *has just arrived. It is an evening in September.*

TATYANA (*in between tears*). И я говорю себе: будь сильной, Татьяна, будь сильной, бывало и хуже; но даже когда умерла моя сестра, мне не было так плохо, как будто мое сердце вырвали и бросили его на пол. [*Pronounced: 'I ja gavaru sebe: bud' sil'noi, buvala i khuzhe; no dazhe kagda umerla maja sestra, mne nebula tak plokha, kakbutta majo sertse vurvali i brosili evo napal.' Meaning: 'And I say to myself: be strong, Tatyana, be strong, you have been through worse, but even my sister died I did not feel this sad, like my heart has been ripped out and thrown on the floor.'*]

TOM. Tatyana, I still haven't learnt any Russian.

TATYANA. I said it is like my heart has been thrown on the floor.

TOM. That's a powerful image.

Pause.

TATYANA. You are late.

TOM. I know I am.

TATYANA. I said to them, 'Wait, we must wait, Tom is coming from America.'

TOM. I missed the ferry.

TATYANA. He will want to be here.

TOM. The demonstrations. It took three hours to get to the port.

TATYANA. It is important for him to be here.

TOM. Thank you, it is.

TATYANA. But they could not change the time of the boat. Everything had been planned.

TOM. I understand.

Pause. She weeps some more.

TATYANA. It is a shame.

TOM. What is?

TATYANA. That you did not stay together. You and Sophia.

TOM. Yes.

TATYANA. You were much good together.

TOM. Yes.

TATYANA. Like butter and jam.

TOM. Was I the butter or the jam?

TATYANA. Like tomato and feta.

TOM. You're making me hungry.

TATYANA. Come, I make you something.

TOM. No, it's fine, I didn't really, I was being… In a while maybe, in a little while.

TATYANA. There is soup.

Pause. She looks around to make sure they are alone.

I prefer you to Sebastian. He is Communist.

TOM. He's all right.

TATYANA. How can you be Communist when you have not lived in Communist country?

TOM. I don't know.

TATYANA. It is easy. I have lived as a child, I know. Nothing works, everything ugly, and people telling you all the time 'Do this, do that.' And if you don't do it, у тебя будут проблемы [*Pronounced: 'utebia budut problemu' Meaning: 'well, you're in trouble'*], you are in trouble.

TOM. Yes.

TATYANA. That is Communism. It is easy being Communist when you are living in the centre of London with beautiful things everywhere: IKEA, Harrods. I do not like him.

TOM. I think he means well.

Pause.

TATYANA. Like butter and jam.

SEBASTIAN *and* LAWRENCE *come on, they are wearing casually smart clothes, maybe jackets.*

TOM. I'm late, I know.

SEBASTIAN. We waited.

LAWRENCE. It was all rather sublime. Apart from that fucking Greek wind.

SEBASTIAN. The *meltemi.*

LAWRENCE. Most of her ended up on the lapels of my Paul Smith jacket but I'm sure that's an honour. She always left her mark.

SEBASTIAN. At least there were not too many waves.

LAWRENCE. Nobody threw up which was a blessing.

TATYANA. At the same place with her father. You remember, Tom?

TOM. Beyond the second bay, yes.

TATYANA. Father and daughter in the sea now. Like fish.

LAWRENCE *and* TOM *hug.*

LAWRENCE. Luke sends his love. He couldn't make it but I told him you were coming.

TOM. How's married life?

LAWRENCE. Married life is good.

Pause.

TATYANA. Where is the girl?

SEBASTIAN. Agatha?

TATYANA. You have forgotten her?

LAWRENCE. She stopped off at the cave. To have a look, she said.

TATYANA. We have to finish the books.

SEBASTIAN. She will come soon and we can start.

TATYANA. So many books.

LAWRENCE. But now we have an extra pair of hands.

TOM. Just tell me what to do.

Pause.

LAWRENCE. We need some more of those boxes.

TATYANA. Come, I take you.

LAWRENCE. Take me, Tatyana, take me.

TATYANA. They are in the room near the kitchen.

LAWRENCE. Lead the way.

TATYANA. And I drop your suitcase in the room, Tom.

She picks up his suitcase and enters the house with LAWRENCE *in tow.*

SEBASTIAN. They said to me... this doctor in Kabul, he spoke beautiful English and he said to me. He said to me it was very quick.

TOM. A bullet in the back of her head.

SEBASTIAN. There were five of them. An ambush.

TOM. I read about it in *The Times*. But some was speculation, the details were vague.

SEBASTIAN. She had only been there two weeks but was already unpopular with some people. The more fundamentalist type.

TOM. The fear. The rage.

SEBASTIAN. It was about education. But for the first time she had a film crew with her. Lately she had become obsessed about the education of girls. From family planning to algebra. So she was doing a piece about three different countries for the BBC. She had done Angola and Pakistan. But from the minute she landed in Afghanistan she was making people quite angry.

TOM. Inevitably.

SEBASTIAN. Rocking the boat, as you say.

TOM. Forever rocking it.

Pause. And then suddenly SEBASTIAN *cries.*

SEBASTIAN. You fucking bastard.

TOM. I'm sorry?

SEBASTIAN. Always living in your fucking shadow.

TOM. Oh.

SEBASTIAN. For some reason she couldn't quite get you out of her system, her mind, I don't know. Not that she spoke about you because she didn't. But I knew, I knew, I knew.

TOM. Okay.

SEBASTIAN. You bastard.

He pulls himself together as quickly and suddenly as he broke down.

I'm sorry. I'm upset.

TOM. We both are.

SEBASTIAN. Some people you never can.

TOM. Never can what?

SEBASTIAN. Shake off…

TOM. No, never.

SEBASTIAN. But I'm glad you came. For her sake. It's what she would have wanted.

TOM. I hope so.

Pause.

SEBASTIAN. It's the grief. It makes you honest.

TOM. It certainly does that.

Pause.

That thing you said. The day we met. You said something about the Towers. You said –

SEBASTIAN. I remember.

TOM. I think you were right.

Pause.

First goes the conviction. Then everything else.

LAWRENCE *and* TATYANA *return, carrying some boxes. They immediately set about packing books in boxes.*

TATYANA. What time are they coming to pick the boxes?

SEBASTIAN. Ten in the morning.

TATYANA. All the books for the girl. Sophie had written especially 'If something happens all my father's books for the girl.'

TOM. What girl?

LAWRENCE. And the house?

SEBASTIAN. It's being sold. At least it'll pay off the debts.

TOM. What will you do, Tatyana?

TATYANA. I will return to Ukraine. My mother says there is some work at her cousin's shop, selling shoes in Horenka.

TOM. If I can do anything.

TATYANA. I leave on Tuesday from Athens to Kiev. My nephew he has arranged me the ticket. He is steward for Air Ukrayina.

TOM. Does he still like Britney Spears?

TATYANA. No. Lady Gaga.

LAWRENCE. Are we just putting these in randomly?

SEBASTIAN. For the time. And maybe we separate when in England. Agatha can take hers to Brighton, the ones she doesn't want I can keep in London.

LAWRENCE. Does she live in a bloody mansion?

SEBASTIAN. I told her I would pay for storage until she leaves university and has somewhere to put them.

TATYANA *has stopped at a particular book, she opens it.*

TATYANA. Ah, look, Tolstoy. He is Russian.

TOM. Indeed.

TATYANA. And Dostoyevsky, and Gogol, and Gorky, and Chekhov and Turgenev. All Russian.

LAWRENCE. A rich tradition.

TATYANA. Always he writes in the book, Edward. Putting the lines under everything.

TOM. Highlighting.

TATYANA. And little pieces of paper. And photographs in the books.

SEBASTIAN. For bookmarks.

TATYANA. Why is he always underlining things. Even in *Anna Karenina*.

TOM. Pointers. Reminders.

AGATHA *walks on but nobody notices her.*

TATYANA. Like here. (*Reads*.) 'I have been seeking an answer to my question but reason could not give it to me. It was life itself that gave me the answer, through my knowledge of good and bad. To love your neighbour could not have been discovered by reason, because it is unreasonable.'

It sounds nicer in Russian.

LAWRENCE *spots* AGATHA.

LAWRENCE. Here she is.

AGATHA. Hello.

LAWRENCE. How was the cave, darling?

AGATHA. Mysterious and a little damp.

LAWRENCE. That's caves for you.

AGATHA. They have built a church around it.

SEBASTIAN. A chapel, yes.

AGATHA. In the beginning it was just a man having dreams in a cave. Then they built a church around it.

SEBASTIAN. We are doing the books and then we will eat something.

AGATHA. I will help you.

TATYANA. I have made the fish stew that Sophie liked.

AGATHA (*spotting* TOM). Hello.

TOM. Hi.

AGATHA. I'm Agatha.

TOM. I am Tom.

TATYANA. Some of these writers have very strange names.

LAWRENCE. You two don't know each other?

TOM. I don't think so.

SEBASTIAN. I think the best thing, Agatha, is just to put them all in the boxes and then separate them in England. Then the ones you don't want I can take.

AGATHA. Until I've read them, I won't know.

LAWRENCE. Ooh, she's a smart one.

TATYANA. Karl Jung. George Steiner.

AGATHA. You are a friend of Sophie's?

TOM. From a long time ago, yes.

TATYANA. Again he has put pen all over it.

LAWRENCE. I'm amazed you've never met.

TATYANA (*reading*). 'Cease being what you are, what biology and circumstance have made you. Become, at the fearful price of abnegation, what you could be.'

TOM. You are a student of Sebastian's?

LAWRENCE. But then, of course, I forget that you and Sophie hadn't seen each other for a long time.

TOM (*covering*). Not for ages.

AGATHA. I am a student, yes, but not of Sebastian's. I have just finished my first year at the University of Sussex, studying Literature and Economics.

TOM. That's an interesting combination.

LAWRENCE. And hopefully a useful one. (*Pulls a face of mock terror.*)

AGATHA. Where are you from, Tom?

TATYANA. What is this word, 'abnegation'?

TOM. I'm from New York.

AGATHA. I've never been to New York.

SEBASTIAN. One day.

AGATHA. But I am a friend of Sophie's too. For a long time, like you.

TATYANA. What does this word mean? Abnegation?

LAWRENCE. I think it means a sacrifice.

TOM. From where?

SEBASTIAN. Like you have to give something up.

TATYANA. Why does he have to write all over the books?

AGATHA. From somewhere far away.

TATYANA. In Russia, this is a crime.

TOM. Whereabouts?

AGATHA. From a town called Amuria. It is about one hundred and forty miles from Kampala in the eastern part of –

TOM. Uganda. I know.

He takes this on board.

AGATHA. You have heard of Amuria?

TOM. I have, yes.

AGATHA. Either Sophie had spoken to you about it or you have a good memory for bad news.

TOM. A little of both.

AGATHA. My town is known for the wrong reasons.

Pause. They carry on going through the books. Apart from TOM, *who can barely move.*

LAWRENCE (*pronouncing it like 'Keats'*). Yeats. Or Yeats. I always forget.

SEBASTIAN (*correctly*). Yeats.

LAWRENCE (*pronouncing it like 'Yeats'*). So then why not Keats? (*Mispronouncing it again.*) 'Ode to a Grecian Urn' by John Keats.

SEBASTIAN. When the boxes are packed we should put them by the kitchen door so that the man picks them straight up from there in the car.

AGATHA (*holding up a book*). This one I want to keep. *The Complete Works of William Shakespeare*.

LAWRENCE. Yes, that's a good one.

TATYANA. Very difficult names. Kierkegaard. Wole Soyinka.

AGATHA. He is from Nigeria.

TATYANA. *Either/Or*. Strange name for a book. *Either/Or*.

AGATHA (*flicking through* The Complete Works). *As You Like It, Twelfth Night or What You Will*.

TATYANA. Paul Tillich, Karen Armstrong, Richard Holloway.

LAWRENCE. You're a lucky girl. What with all the libraries being closed down it's a good time to inherit one.

SEBASTIAN. Come, we start moving the boxes to the back of the kitchen. Then we can clear the terrace for dinner.

TATYANA. And I bring the fish soup.

AGATHA. *Romeo and Juliet, Hamlet, Othello*.

LAWRENCE (*picking up a box*). I'll take this one. Oooh, my hernia.

AGATHA. *Cymbeline, The Winter's Tale, The Tempest*.

She puts it carefully in a box and returns to packing the remaining books.

LAWRENCE, SEBASTIAN and TATYANA all go off carrying some of the boxes of books. The space starts to clear.

AGATHA and TOM are left alone. They are silent for a while. Then TOM speaks.

TOM. And how did you. What I mean is. How did you. Meet Sophie. How did she meet you.

AGATHA. When I was eight years old Sophie came to write a piece about the organisation which was helping us raise funds for the Fletcher case… Ten years ago.

TOM. And you were. I mean. One of the. You were affected by the events of?

AGATHA. My sister died but I was lucky. I was paralysed down the right side of my body for three or four years and it is still what I call 'my lazy half', but yes, I was one of what they came to call the Fletcher children.

TOM. The Fletcher children.

AGATHA. Afterwards, everyone packed up and left. But from the beginning Sophie was more involved. 'Hands-on', isn't that what you say?

TOM. Hands-on.

AGATHA. When she first came she lived in our house for a few weeks and became close to my parents. She seemed to have a purpose to be there. But then she was one of those people.

TOM. One of those people?

AGATHA. Who lived with some sense of purpose, I mean.

TOM. Yes.

AGATHA. So she became close to us and then it was she who paid for me to go to the International School in Kampala and then has helped me to come here to follow my higher education. Not only financially.

TOM. It was kind of her.

AGATHA. But she would be very angry if you called it charity. She does not believe in charity, she always said. As long as you see it as charity, things will never change.

TOM. No.

AGATHA. It is more than that. Something else.

TOM. Something else?

AGATHA. Maybe a different way of seeing.

TOM (*almost to himself*). Nothing is abstract.

AGATHA *stands up and picks up the box.*

AGATHA. I will take the box to put it with the others.

She leaves, carrying the box. TOM *is left alone onstage. He is reeling. There is a gesture, something like a hand to the face, a lowering of the head which looks almost as if he might be in physical pain, as if he is finding it hard to breathe.*

Then LAWRENCE *returns with* TATYANA.

TATYANA. Another five minutes and the stew is ready.

LAWRENCE. The last few to go and then we're finished. Come on, Tats, give us a hand.

They return to putting the last few books into the remaining boxes. They both look at them one by one as they put them into the boxes.

Graham Greene: *The End of the Affair.* Oh, that was a good one, despite the whole Catholic thing. But I enjoyed it. Julianne Moore was the best thing in it.

TATYANA. And then afterwards maybe we have watermelon.

LAWRENCE. Maya Angelou, oh, bless her, Goddess Maya. Dickens, Dickens, Dickens, three Dickens in a row, I'm sure that was planned. e.e. cummings. George Eliot, E.M. Forster, Gabriel García Márquez, George Eliot, Plato's *Republic*, *The Kama Sutra*? Oh, well, an eclectic collection.

TATYANA. And then I make coffee.

AGATHA *and* SEBASTIAN *return.*

SEBASTIAN. One more box each and then we finish.

AGATHA. I will do these ones over here.

They join LAWRENCE *and* TATYANA *in piling away the books. For a short while, as they work, nobody talks.*

TOM. And when was the last time you saw her, Agatha? Sophie, I mean.

AGATHA. I was lucky. Over the Easter break I went to stay with her in London for a week. It was just the two of us.

SEBASTIAN. I was in Chile, visiting my mother.

AGATHA. For that week she was not working. Just before she went to Afghanistan. We stayed up at night and talked a lot, maybe had what you might call philosophical conversations.

TOM. Philosophical conversations?

AGATHA. About life, really, and about religion too. Things I could never really talk to my own parents about.

TOM. Couldn't you?

AGATHA. My parents are not educated, you see. They can read and write but that is about all. The only book they know is the Bible.

LAWRENCE. Speaking of which, I found this one earlier.

He leans over and picks up an old book, hands it to AGATHA. *She holds on to it until the end of the scene.*

AGATHA. Thank you.

LAWRENCE. An old King James.

TATYANA. It is Edward's.

LAWRENCE. And there's a Koran in that one there. (*Points to another box.*)

AGATHA. So they revere it and you cannot say anything against it. It would upset them. I think it is natural.

TOM. Very.

AGATHA. But with Sophie we could talk about other things, and all these other books too, other stories. So yes, we talked a lot, sometimes well into the night.

LAWRENCE. She certainly liked talking.

SEBASTIAN (*looking at the book he is holding*). Cervantes.

They carry on sorting the books.

TATYANA. Look. Look at us. I am from the Ukraine. You are from Chile. Tom is American. You are African. And you are from Croydon. We are the globalisation.

SEBASTIAN (*putting the last few books in the box*). Nearly there.

AGATHA. One night we were talking about Christianity.

LAWRENCE. Nothing on the telly then?

AGATHA. Edward her father was a bishop, you know.

TOM. I did know that, yes.

AGATHA. But, by all accounts, an unconventional bishop.

TOM. Definitely unconventional.

LAWRENCE. He fought our cause within the Church.

SEBASTIAN. Pablo Neruda, in the original.

AGATHA. Well, one night I said to her – asked her – how she must have been shaped by him. By his Christianity. I said, 'Do you consider yourself a Christian, Sophie?'

TOM. And what did she say?

AGATHA. She said, no, she wasn't a Christian. When she was a child, maybe, but not any more. And then she used the funniest expression to describe herself.

LAWRENCE. And what was that?

AGATHA. She said: 'I am a faith machine.'

TOM. What did she mean?

AGATHA. She said of course Darwin was right, we had crawled out of our caves on all fours, and then slowly, painfully, risen onto our back legs and stood up and yes, yes we were still 'red in tooth and claw' – Don't look surprised, Lawrence, I did Tennyson for my A-level.

LAWRENCE. Oh, hark at her.

AGATHA. Anyway, she said that yes we had evolved from that but that somewhere along the line some people – and she said she was one of them – had inherited in their machinery something that made them need to believe. And when I said, 'Yes, but what is it you believe in?', she just replied, 'Against all empirical evidence and rational enquiry I continue to believe in the human being.'

SEBASTIAN. Finished.

SEBASTIAN *closes his box and picks it up. They have all finished packing their boxes. Except for* AGATHA *who has a few books left.*

110

TATYANA. Come, we take them. And then we go and get the soup. It will be delicious… Lawrence, you bring the plates.

LAWRENCE. Yes, ma'am.

TATYANA. And, Sebastian, you open some wine. And we have the toast. To Sophie.

SEBASTIAN. Agatha?

AGATHA. I'm coming.

There are just a handful of books left and TOM *helps put them into* AGATHA*'s box. She is still holding the Bible which she now starts to look at. The rest are making their way into the house.*

LAWRENCE (*to* TATYANA). Why do you keep looking at me like that?

TATYANA. Like what?

LAWRENCE. Like the way you are now.

TATYANA. You know it is funny. Many years ago, this man was here, a friend of Edward's from Kenya. You look very like him.

LAWRENCE. Wonderful, so you're a racist.

TATYANA. I am not racist. I like the Africans, the Japanese and even some of the gays.

LAWRENCE. How enlightened of you.

TATYANA. The only ones I don't like are the Communists.

LAWRENCE. So you don't think it's racist to say that I look exactly like the only other black man you've ever spoken to?

TATYANA. He was your spitting brother.

SEBASTIAN. Why don't you like the Communists?

TATYANA. My grandmother she is the only good Communist I know.

SEBASTIAN. Oh, so there is a good one, is there?

TATYANA. She says to me you can only be a Communist with the heart. And then she says we are not ready yet.

LAWRENCE. Not evolved.

AGATHA. Maybe one day.

LAWRENCE. That's hopeful.

SEBASTIAN. So in the meantime we keep looking.

LAWRENCE. And eating.

TATYANA. Come for the soup.

TATYANA, LAWRENCE and SEBASTIAN leave, carrying the last boxes.

Except for AGATHA's. TOM puts the last few books into it. She is still leafing through the Bible.

AGATHA. I cannot take the Bible word for word like my parents. I know that when it says something about – I don't know – eating pork, or about slaves or the gay people – my goodness, there are so many gay people in Brighton! – I realise it is very much part of the time it was written in. The times are like shedding skins. But what lies behind them, that lasts for ever.

TOM. The heart of the story.

AGATHA. Do unto others as you would have them do unto you.

TOM. The Golden Rule.

AGATHA. Don't hide you light under a bushel, Tom!

TOM. Stick it on your head?

AGATHA. Or my favourite.

TOM. Which is?

AGATHA. For what good shall it profit a man shall he gain the whole world?

TOM. Yes, that is a good one.

She looks out at the view from the terrace.

AGATHA. It is so beautiful here.

TOM. This is the time of day.

AGATHA. But there is a chill in the air.

TOM. September.

Pause.

AGATHA. I'm sorry, I didn't…

TOM. You didn't what?

AGATHA. I know you are from New York and that you were a
friend of Sophie's but the thing is you didn't really say.

TOM. I didn't say what?

AGATHA. This will sound very rude.

TOM. I can take it.

AGATHA. Because you didn't really say how. And I don't think
Sophie had mentioned you, so I think what I'm asking is…

She thinks how she can phrase it.

Who are you, Tom?

TOM. Oh. Me? Let's see. Em. Now that's an interesting question.
Who am I?

Pause.

I was. She and I. We were. Now, let's see.

He thinks long and hard.

The missing man. Let's call me the missing man.

AGATHA *looks at him, puzzled. She smiles.*

*She closes the Bible and places it carefully into the box with the
other books.*

Then, at a distance, SOPHIE *appears. Like* EDWARD *in the first
scene, she is an apparition.*

She stands at a short distance from TOM *and* AGATHA *and
looks at them. They cannot see her but her presence is felt.*

AGATHA *and* TOM *close the box of books.*

Blackout.

The End.

A Nick Hern Book

The Faith Machine first published in Great Britain as a paperback original in 2011 by Nick Hern Books Limited, 14 Larden Road, London W3 7ST, in association with the Royal Court Theatre, London

Cover image: Pablo Bernasconi
Cover design: Ned Hoste, 2H

Typeset by Nick Hern Books, London
Printed and bound by CPI Group (UK) Ltd, Croydon, CR0 4YY

A CIP catalogue record for this book is available from the British Library

ISBN   978 1 84842 217 9

MIX
Paper from
responsible sources
FSC® C020852